MAGIC IN THE DESERT

By

Dan Perry

Magic in the Desert
by Dan Perry

Copyright © 2015 Frank Thayer and Mike Waldner
All rights reserved including print, online, and film/video
Permission granted to publish excerpts only as per Title 17 of the
U.S. Copyright Act of 1976

ISBN # 978-0-692-49717-3

Photos and Illustrations in this book published with permission of the New Mexico State University Library Archives and Special Collections and from print and online archives of the NMSU yearbook Swastika, 1900-1961

Cover design created by Mario Lara
Book design created by Pamela Porter

Printed by: LithExcel Communication, Albuquerque, N.M.

Magic in the Desert Committee, Publishers
c/o Frank Thayer
P.O. Box 3136 UPB
Las Cruces, NM 88003
http://www.magicinthedesert60.com

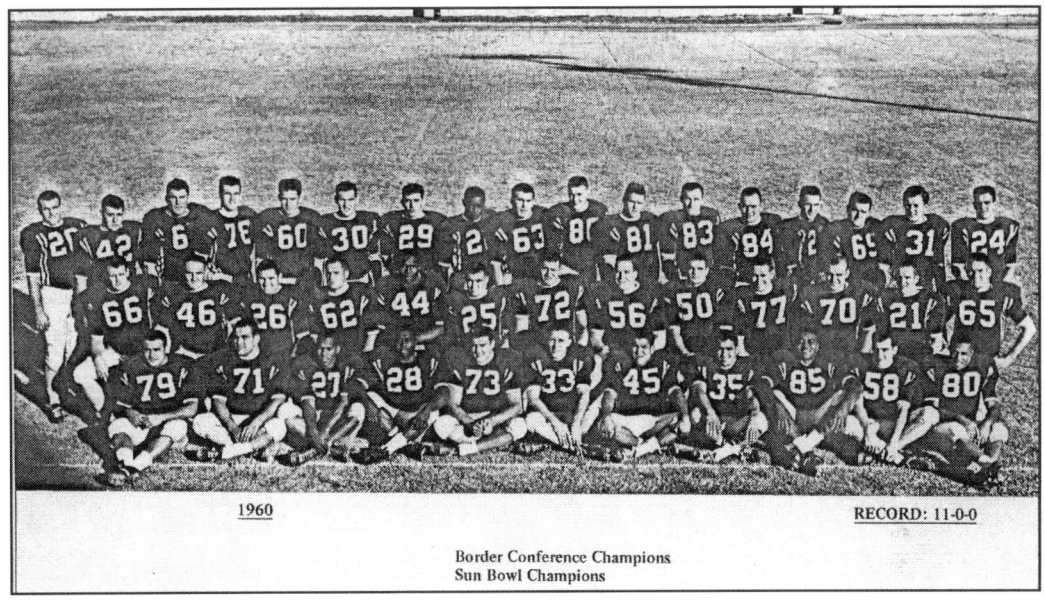

1960
RECORD: 11-0-0
Border Conference Champions
Sun Bowl Champions

First Row:
Jerry Gambatese, Clem Mancini, Pervis Atkins, Bob Gaiters, Lou Zivkovich, Charley Johnson, Sal Gonzalez, Ricky Alba, Bob Kelly, Jim Worrick, E.A. Sims
Second Row:
J.W. Witt, Morris Hodgson, Chris Cadenhead, Ken Hays, Bob Jackson, Doug Veazey, Don Yannessa, Carl Covington, Bill Wallace, Floyd Strickland, Jack Moss, Bob Langford, Jim Campbell
Third Row:
Gary Hobbs, Tony Calabria, Ralph Leonard, Mike Rutherford, Dennis Ganstine, Lonnie Carter, Frank Cusenza, Charles Pettes, Allan Sepkowitz, Ron Logback, Royce Cassell, Pete Smolanovich, Bill Birdwell, Dave Thompson, John Shamburg, Don Rierson, Armando Alba (NMSU Yearbook photo)

Dedicated to the spirit of New Mexico A&M College and New Mexico State University and the gridiron heroes of almost 120 years exemplified by that perfect season of 1960. Team members living and departed still hear the echo of the cheers.

Contents

FOREWORD
INTRODUCTION
PROLOGUE
1960 ROSTER
PREFACE/THE WAY IT WAS IN 1960

CHAPTER ONE: In the Beginning — 1894-1928
CHAPTER TWO: In the Beginning — Hold on to your hat: 110 to 3
CHAPTER THREE: In the Beginning — The Rentfrows
CHAPTER FOUR: In the Beginning — The Hines Years 1928-1939
CHAPTER FIVE: In the Beginning — Sun Bowl 1936
CHAPTER SIX: In the Beginning — 1940-1957
CHAPTER SEVEN: Warren Woodson's Resume
CHAPTER EIGHT: Setting the Foundation — 1958
CHAPTER NINE: Setting the Foundation — 1959
CHAPTER TEN: Setting the Foundation — Sun Bowl 1959
CHAPTER ELEVEN: 1960 — The Perfect Season
  • 1960 Aggie Statistical Leaders
CHAPTER TWELVE: Sun Bowl 1960
CHAPTER THIRTEEN: Decline and Departure — 1961-1967
CHAPTER FOURTEEN: The Sanctions
CHAPTER FIFTEEN: The Rest of the Way — 1968-2014
CHAPTER SIXTEEN: Yesterday, Today, Tomorrow

EPILOGUE/A CHANCE MEETING
ACKNOWLEDGMENTS
INDEX

Foreword

I welcome you to walk down the NMSU football memory lane.

It was my husband Dan's dream that this book be written to honor the undefeated 1960 team and perhaps instruct students and student-athletes of today about the skills and teamwork that made that squad so famous in the annals of NMSU history.

Dan and I met in a philosophy course at NMSU in the fall of 1961, and became college sweethearts. Dan was commissioned a second lieutenant in the U.S. Army right before graduation in 1962. He was one of 24 to get a gold bar with his diploma that year. We married that August, and were off for the ride of my life as a wife and mother of a military family. Dan spent his career serving his country and attained the rank of colonel before retiring.

Each year, as August gave way to September, no matter where we were stationed in the world, Dan's mind would drift back to campus. He would wonder aloud how his dear Aggies would do that upcoming season. He absolutely loved college football, but it was tough being an alumnus come fall since the NMSU teams, after the stunning 11-0 year, never again attained the same heights.

After his tour in Vietnam in 1970, the Army sent Dan to the University of Alabama to get a master's degree in journalism. Our two kids, Alan and Cindy, grew up with Dan teaching them about the game and how to love winning — with the Crimson Tide — and how to accept mostly defeat with the Aggies.

It's funny, but Dan would never really get bitter when he knew the Aggies would have yet another down season. He would just sort of go into a wishful mode, whistle the fight song, and wonder, "When? When would there be another great season or string of seasons?"

He would wax nostalgically about Charley Johnson, Bob Gaiters and Pervis Atkins, and the beautiful passing, running, blocking and tackling he remembered. For a brief moment or two, he'd be right back on campus under A Mountain in the press box charting a game so he could call in his story to Buck Lanier at the *El Paso Times*.

Dan loved to relive those days. When Buck was working for the *Long Beach Press-Telegram* in California and was covering the war in Saigon, he and Dan got together and reminisced all the more. Dan's childhood friend Charlie Rogers always served as a sounding board for him to critique the gridiron play. And what a thrill it was for us to have Pervis Atkins present when we celebrated our 25th wedding anniversary. Having Pervis there to party and celebrate and sing the fight song with us was simply special.

We retired from the military in 1989 and settled in San Antonio, and as the years passed ESPN started to provide more regional coverage of college football. Dan never missed an NMSU game that was broadcast.

Over the years, the memory of that desert magic in 1960, that miraculous football team, kept tugging at his heart. He wished someone would write a book about the team. When no one stepped forward, he decided it should be his assignment. After his second retirement from his second profession, family and marriage counseling, he knew his calling was to write a book about Aggie football and that enchanting time in Las Cruces. He began researching and lining up interviews.

In 2013, cancer kept Dan from seeing the completion of his dear project, which grew to include the highs and lows of Aggie football from 1894 to 2014. Mike Waldner, Frank Thayer, his college roommates, and Charlie Rogers have generously completed *Magic in the Desert* for him.

As you read about the great seasons in Aggie football history, consider the question: Why not again?

— Irene Perry 2015

Introduction

A magic football season in New Mexico is treasured for its rarity just as New Mexico values and conserves its water resources. In some way, there is a parallel between the state's attention to its most valued substance and a New Mexico State University football team whose astounding performance captured the attention of the nation in 1960.

The Rio Grande River begins its 1,885-mile journey to the Gulf of Mexico high in the San Juan Mountains of Southwestern Colorado. The headwaters in the Four Corners collect and start the flow of the precious moisture, and these streams create the Rio Grande that meanders east before taking an abrupt right turn and heading south, bisecting the Land of Enchantment.

The river passes north to south through the Rio Grande Gorge near Taos and then accepts what the Chama River has to offer near Española. While skirting Santa Fe, about 20 miles to the west, these legendary waters flow through the state's largest city, Albuquerque, where the Interstate 40 bridge spans a three-quarter-mile channel.

Elephant Butte Dam and Caballo Dam have provided important flood control and irrigation south of Albuquerque and north of Las Cruces since construction was completed in 1916. The now-regulated river reaches the Mesilla Valley about 35 miles north of Las Cruces, eventually finding Texas, where it provides a common border for the United States with Mexico in its journey to the Gulf of Mexico.

The Mesilla Valley is characterized by its few remaining bosques, the groves of brush and trees surviving in the flood plain of the river, as well as native cottonwood trees and invasive tamarisk, known locally as salt cedar. Agriculture is critical to the people of the valley. Stahmam Farms, one of the world's larges pecan orchards, is located south of Las Cruces. Cotton, chile, onions and corn are other important cash crops grown in the valley. Cottonwood trees towering along the riverbanks in and around Las Cruces are among the continent's largest. The trees can grow up to 80 feet tall and live to be over 100 years old. The name comes from the most recognizable feature, a small, fluffy, almost lighter-than-air white seed ball an inch in diameter that is released by the female tree in early summer. This fluff carries in the breeze and so much "cotton" is released during the fluff blizzard that it can drift into piles that are very much like snow.

A stand of cottonwoods along the west bank of the Rio Grande south of the I-10 and U.S. Highway 70 bridges have provided a gathering place for generations of New Mexico State University students. The university's fight song includes the phrase "And when we win this game, we'll buy a keg of booze…And we'll drink it to the Aggies 'til we wobble in our shoes!" Win or lose, one of the most memorable places to accomplish the drinking to the fight song was a place on the river at what came to be referred to as "The Drinkin' Tree."

The Drinkin' Tree was not necessarily one particular tree but any cottonwood tree where the keg or kegs wound up, usually on a weekend afternoon in the days before tailgate parties were invented. The longer the day got, the drier the keg, or kegs, became, and the louder the songs, the more inventive became the touch football contests, the baseball or softball games. Many of the pickup football games ended up in the river itself. I've often wondered if any of the Drinkin' Tree crowd went missing, maybe during the late spring snow runoffs in Colorado and Northern New Mexico, when the river was higher and faster, and had to be fished out of the Gulf by a U.S. Coast Guard cutter!

Oh, I know the Rio Grande. I also know the cottonwood tree.

As a senior U.S. Army officer stationed at the Pentagon in the early '80s, I went into the building's health clinic for my routine annual physical. I was called back the following day by the phone call: "We're going to have to retake your chest x-ray. We think a water spot got on the one we took yesterday."

The day after that, another call: "We're making you an appointment at Walter Reed. It wasn't a water spot. There's something abnormal going on."

A few weeks later, after retrieving previous x-rays from my former assignment in Germany, I marched in to my appointment. The diagnosis? "Here's the spot on the Pentagon's x-ray. Nothing in the same spot from your German x-rays. Something is growing there that we can watch over the next couple of months, or we can take it out."

A few days later when I awoke in post-op, having opted to "take it out," my surgeon was hovering over me. "Were you raised on the Rio Grande?" was his question.

"Yes, raised in Albuquerque and went to school in Las Cruces, but why do you ask?"

The doctor went on: "Pathology came back on your 'tumor.' It was the spore of a cottonwood tree!" I apparently had, at some time in the previous 39 years, inhaled one of those fuzzy, fluffy, floating cottonwood seeds. The upper lobe of my right lung had been incubating a seed from "The Drinkin' Tree."

Yes, I know the Rio Grande. I know cottonwood trees and seeds! And I was blessed to be a student witness to the only two Aggie football teams to complete at least eight wins during the season against college teams. The 1959 squad went 8-3 by virtue of its Sun Bowl win over North Texas State while the 1960 team won its 10 regular season games and tacked on an 11th win in NMSU's second consecutive Sun Bowl appearance.

There were no eight-win seasons before 1959 and no eight-win seasons since 1960. There were no bowl invites from 1961 through 2012, the longest dry streak in the country at this writing. (The disheartening streak has continued unabated through the 2014 season.) The 1959-1960 seasons were equivalent to a monster monsoon drenching NMSU with victory in the midst of a continuing desert drought.

Was 1960 really magic, as Pervis Atkins opined, that made it happen? Was it Warren Woodson's coaching abilities? Was it divine inspiration? Was it superior athletes? Maybe a weak schedule? Blind luck? Was there an unusual willingness to sacrifice that put it all together? Clusters of friendships that characterized the team? Team maturity? High player graduation rates that followed the season? It could be the combination of several of these elements. Whatever "it" was, I'm fired up enough to head back to "The Drinkin' Tree" to figure all this out.

—Dan Perry 2012

Editor's note: Dan Perry, a Fort Sumner, New Mexico native, died on March 9, 2013 in San Antonio, Texas.

Aggie Memorial Stadium in 1957 (Courtesy of New Mexico State University Archives and Special Collections Department)

1960 Roster

Armando Alba — freshman tailback, Deming, New Mexico

Ricky Alba — senior safety, quarterback, Deming, New Mexico

Pervis Atkins — senior wingback-tailback, Oakland, California

Bill Birdwell — freshman defensive end, fullback, Clayton, New Mexico

Chris Cadenhead — junior defensive back, Amarillo, Texas

Tony Calabria — sophomore wingback, Aliquippa, Pennsylvania

Jim Campbell — junior guard, Hobbs, New Mexico

Lonnie Carter-Terry — sophomore quarterback, Compton, California

Royce Cassell — junior end, Pecos, Texas

Carl Covington — junior center, San Antonio, Texas

Frank Cusenza — junior cornerback, Ceres, California

Bob Gaiters — senior tailback, Zanesville, Ohio

Jerry Gambatese — senior tackle, Burbank, California

Dennis Ganstine — freshman center, Harlingen, Texas

Sal Gonzalez — senior fullback, Anthony, New Mexico

Ken Hays — junior guard, San Antonio, Texas

Gary Hobbs —freshman tailback, Amarillo, Texas

Morris Hodgson — junior safety, De Kalb, Texas

Bob Jackson — junior fullback, Palm Springs, California

Charley Johnson — senior quarterback, Big Spring, Texas

Bob Kelly — senior end, Carlsbad, New Mexico

Bob Langford — junior linebacker, Pampa, Texas

Ralph Leonard — freshman guard, Crystal Lake, Illinois

Ron Logback — junior end, Antonito, Colorado

Clem Mancini — senior tackle, El Paso, Texas

Jack Moss — junior tackle, Salina, Kansas

Charles Pettes — junior tailback, Las Cruces, New Mexico

Don Rierson — freshman quarterback, Las Cruces, New Mexico

Mike Rutherford — freshman tackle, Kingsville, Texas

Allan Sepkowitz — junior guard, Amarillo, Texas

John Shamburg — sophomore guard, Creighton, Pennsylvania

E.A. Sims — senior end, Abilene, Texas

Pete Smolanovich — junior end, Poland, Ohio

Floyd Strickland — junior tackle, Hobbs, New Mexico

Dave Thompson — sophomore wingback, Tarentum, Pennsylvania

Doug Veazey — junior cornerback, Amarillo, Texas

Bill Wallace — junior center, San Antonio, Texas

J.W. Witt — junior guard, Amarillo, Texas

Jim Worrick — senior center, Philadelphia, Pennsylvania

Don Yannessa — junior tackle, Aliquippa, Pennsylvania

Browning Yelvington — senior end, Omaha, Nebraska

Lou Zivkovich — senior tackle, Rankin, Penslvania

(Hometowns are based on where the players went to high school with one possible exception, that being Ralph Leonard. There is insufficient information to be sure about him.)

Prologue

The Arizona State Sun Devils had just put their home crowd into a frenzy by going up on the New Mexico State Aggies 24-14 early in the fourth quarter. I sat sullen in the press box on the west sidelines in the old Sun Devil Stadium. My press buddy, Las Cruces *Sun-News* sports editor Abe Perilman sat beside me, shaking his head, his ever-present pipe wagging back and forth between his lips. Less than a quarter to go and our 10-game winning streak on the line. I was starting to get sick.

Here comes the ASU kickoff and what I've replayed in my mind for over 50 years. Pervis Atkins gathers the ball on his own 2-yard line, starts up the west sidelines and heads north. I've used my extended right arm at the diagonal with thumb pointed up to represent Perv. I still see his crimson number 27 on the white road game jersey, and the same number penned on my thumb. He's on the 20 ... the 25 ... the 40. Key blocks seem to be working as I stand up and start pounding on Perilman's shoulder.

Perv and my thumb are now directly below the press box, gliding along as he avoids tackles. One last lunging Sun Devil misses. Perv breezes past our 250 or so Aggie fans in the ground level seats on the west side as he sprints into the end zone. Now it's 24-20, and we miss the extra point kick. Atkins made that 98-yard trip much faster than it takes to read this description.

We kick off, and hold the Devils, forcing them to punt. We start our big comeback with a fumble. The Devils recover on our 15 ... game over. Damn! The Devils slowly, slowly eat up the time, keeping their game on the ground. They are down to the Aggies' 2, and I'm starting to get sick again. The Devils fumble, and we recover on our 4-yard line! Abe knocks over his coffee in the excitement surrounding the scramble for the ball.

Pervis carries the ball. There's a penalty. The ball is placed on the 3. Now, I can hold out my right arm again at a right diagonal, my 27 thumb pointed up. Backs in position deep in our own end zone with time running out, it's a pitchout to ... Pervis, number 27. He skirts his left end, gains 15 and starts reversing field, dodging and junking his way up the east sideline, right in front of the ASU Sun Devil bench. I am pounding on Perilman again, and he spills his cup of coffee again while my thumb tracks Perv as he travels north ... 50 ... 40 ... 30 ... until the tacklers catch him at their 26! Count 'em ... 71 yards. It's now someone else's turn to get sick!

The Aggies drive down the remaining yards to the ASU 3, and a quarterback Charley Johnson toss to end Bob Kelly put the receiver in the end zone doing consecutive back flips in the pandemonium that ensued. The extra point is good: Aggies 27, Sun Devils 24, with 3:51 left to play. This time it really is game over. Yes! Eleven straight wins over the past two years. I help Abe clean up the coffee on the bench as he adjusts the pipe in his mouth, and then I apologize to the Arizona sports writers in the booth for being less than objective in my own behavior. I then file my story with The El Paso Times and it is time to party.

The following Tuesday, Atkins was named AP Back of the Week for the nation, an honor that may have helped him earn All-American recognition at season's end and, 49 years later in 2009, induction into the College Football Hall of Fame.

The Aggies 16-game winning streak ended with the second game of the 1961 season, but the Aggie magic was already legend by then.

* * *

In February 2009, the 1960 undefeated New Mexico State University football team was inducted into the school's Sports Hall of Fame. During festivities associated with the induction, Atkins was interviewed and asked what had made that team so special. Pervis didn't hesitate: "It was like magic, man ... magic in the desert!"

Pervis was right ... absolutely right. Everything about that 1960 season was magic. I was classified as a junior at NMSU that fall semester of 1960 and witnessed "magic in the desert" first hand. I've waited all these years for someone to actually tell the story of that magical time. However, when no one stepped up to the plate, I pledged that I would try to capture the spirit of that time. Knowing that the story couldn't be told without every remaining member of the team and staff having been offered the opportunity to add his or her own part of the magical equation.

The magic started to build in the spring of 1958 with the arrival on what was then the New Mexico A&M College campus of Coach Warren Woodson, who came to Las Cruces from the University of Arizona. Prior to Woodson's arrival, New Mexico A&M College had gone through 17 seasons with 16 losing records. Six of the seven head coaches immediately preceding Woodson left with losing records. And while his '58 squad finished with a losing 4-6 record (17 losing records in 18 seasons, if you're counting), the losing tide turned the following year with an 8-3 finish, including an improbable Sun Bowl win on the last day of the year.

That final win was a harbinger of the perfect season to come. The 1960 season was an unblemished 11-0 record with a second consecutive Sun Bowl victory following the season. The fortune at one time "football-poor" A&M changed 180 degrees along with the change of the school name to New Mexico State University that same year.

I found my way to New Mexico A&M in 1957 following my graduation from Highland High School in Albuquerque. I had explored going to Texas A&M with some of my Highland buddies but discovered the reality of average grades, a mediocre SAT composite score, no hope of any kind of a scholarship, and out-of-state tuition costs. I needed to get out of town, so I set my sights on Las Cruces.

New Mexico A&M wasn't completely unknown to me and my family. My mother's next older brother, Roy "Bud" Skipworth, had attended New Mexico A&M in the last 1930s and early '40s. Pearl Harbor pushed Uncle Buddy and thousands like him into the military's "90 Day Wonder" commissioning program for officers. He was later killed on Okinawa while participating in his fourth combat campaign. While growing up in Albuquerque, my stepdad had attended the University of New Mexico in the late 1940s and early 1950s, the school that dominated the football Aggies year after year during those years.

I went off to Las Cruces with my Fort Sumner childhood friend Charlie Rogers. While driving to Cruces, via my hometown of Fort Sumner, I decided I was going to declare journalism as my major. I had visions of sports reporting and sugar plums dancing in my head by the end of our 260-mile trip.

My first writing experience came with the weekly Las Cruces *Herald*, although my janitorial responsibilities there probably blinded my editors to my talent at the time. In the spring of 1959, I was offered the job of part-time "stringer" for The El Paso *Times* as a regional correspondent for the campus and local community. This position eventually got me into the press box at Aggie Memorial Stadium and paid for the majority of my tuition and books for the next three years. I covered the Las Cruces scene and routinely reported local obituaries along with junior high, high school and college sports from 1958 into the summer of 1962.

Additionally, I did some sports reporting for the Las Cruces *Sun-News* when sports editor Perilman was on vacation. I landed the job of sports editor for the college yearbook, the *Swastika*, for three years starting with the 1960 edition. I also was sports editor for the university newspaper, *The Round Up*, in my senior year, 1961-62.

At graduation, when I was awarded my bachelor's degree in journalism, I was commissioned as a lieutenant in the U.S. Army, thanks to some U.S. Army Reserve time plus four years in the land grant school's Army ROTC program.

As another graduation bonus, I married my college sweetheart Irene Elizabeth Caranta, of Monero, N.M., whose father and twin brother had attended A&M in 1930-31. They both played multiple sports for the Aggies. My branch of commission was in the Army's Military Police Corps; so Irene and I were to experience 22 moves in 27 years on active duty.

I had four journalism-related assignments during my active duty years. The Army assigned me as editor of *The Military Police Journal* at Fort Gordon, Ga. for two years, from 1972-74, after sending me to the University of Alabama to get my master's in journalism. Later, I was assigned from 1982-84 to the Office of the Chief, Army Public Affairs in the Pentagon in Washington, D.C. From the Pentagon, we were sent to Texas, where I took over as Chief, Public Affairs, 5th Army at Fort Sam Houston, San Antonio, Texas for 18 months and from there as Chief, Public affairs, U.S. Army Western Command at Fort Shafter, Hawaii (a real hardship assignment!).

In the early '90s, we returned to San Antonio to start our retirement home and second job search. Irene, who had gone back to school while I was in Vietnam, earned her bachelor's in education in 1971 from UNM and, later, a master's in special education from the University of Hawaii in 1989. She was very quickly able to get a job teaching at the high school level when we established our San Antonio residence.

I wasn't interested in carrying a gun on my hip after retirement, but I did not find a journalism or community relations job in San Antonio, so I took advantage of my G.I. Bill and earned a second master's degree, in counseling, from St. Mary's University. Irene retired from teaching in 2003, and she told me she planned to travel. Of course, she asked what my plans were. I transferred my clients to other superb therapists and gladly joined Irene to seek our adventures in distant places.

In the 52 years since my beloved Aggie football team went undefeated it has become increasingly clear magic indeed happened in the desert 1960, and I know because I kept a close eye on the NMSU sports scene.

I have thrilled at the Aggie basketball teams as they have repeatedly returned to the NCAA "Big Dance." The ladies' volleyball team has been ultra-competitive since the team's inception. The women's swim team is in the process of building a powerhouse, having placed third and then second in the Western Athletic Conference Swimming and Diving Championships in 2009 and 2010. Aggie golf teams have brought much glory to the NMSU athletic department, while the baseball and softball teams have shown flashes of promise throughout the years.

On the other hand, my Crimson and White heart has been bludgeoned, bloodied and bruised since the late 1960s and the departure of Coach Woodson by what has come to be called by some so-called experts as "the worst college football team" of the year/decade/century (pick one). From 1968 to 2012, the Aggies compiled a 144-353-3 win-loss-tie record, including four winning seasons in those 45 years. I have yearned for a return to my student years, when Aggie football whose achievements were a marvel to experience – a time when there was a steady diet of good coaching, rushing titles, accurate passing, gifted student athletes and gridiron victories.

And so I want to tell the story of the magic that struck NMSU so long ago. The selfish part of me in writing this book is to challenge my memory of what happened. I have waited and waited for this story to be fully told or retold. I am also eager to get this project completed for the teammates … for their own versions of the incredible events that impacted their own lives as they made history for their university. This is also being written as validation for wives of the players who may not have personally witnessed the magic, but who are reminded of it as the stories are passed to their children and grandchildren.

– Dan Perry 2012

Preface
The way it was in 1960

In my most recent visit to NMSU, the bustle of the campus reminded me that it was home to just over 17,500 students, a far cry from my student days in 1960, when we thought it crowded with just over 3,315 students; and the campus was outgrowing its facilities. Enrollment jumped that year, over the 2,862 students of 1959.

Aerial view of Aggie Stadium, pictured at far right. (Courtesy of New Mexico State University Archives and Special Collections Department)

I did a lot of walking all over campus in those days, much of it with my bride-to-be Irene. Now, my memories may be challenged (we know that all memories can be distorted by time), but I've checked the major points with my old NMSU buddies Charlie Rogers, Frank Thayer, Mike Waldner and others so that we can freeze in time for a moment Las Cruces and the university as it existed in that magical year.

If we start with Aggie Memorial Stadium, the tower still stands just as it did when it was the sentinel to the west of the field, with its press box and concrete bleachers. The gridiron was on the north-south axis. Solano Drive came right down to the parking lot in those days. Conveniently, Williams gymnasium was located right beside the stadium along University Avenue. I remember that the facilities were bare bones, as the team members often did weight training underneath the bleachers, shielded from the Las Cruces sun in August.

Most of our classes were in the buildings around the Horseshoe, dominated by the administration building, Hadley Hall. That building has changed very little, but it once housed the entire administration offices, including the president and vice president upstairs, registrar, the business office and the dean of students on the main floor and the U.S. Post Office in the basement. Tucked away in the northeast corner

Milton Student Center in the mid-1950s, taken from the desert between Breland and Garcia dormitories. (Courtesy of New Mexico State University Archives and Special Collections Department)

of the basement was the two-man public relations office staffed by PR chief Dave Rodwell and sports guy Dick Mullins.

Students routinely were in and out of Hadley on a daily basis since the post office was our main connection with home. After all most of us did not have telephone access, and a call to my hometown of Ft. Sumner was long distance and a rare occurrence.

As a journalism major, many of my classes were in the Young Hall English Department, beside one of the two fountains east of Hadley. Today, that building houses both Army and Air Force ROTC. The sidewalk east of Hadley led past the dirt faculty parking lot behind Young Hall and directly to Milton Hall. Here was the real nerve center of the student side of the campus, before Corbett Center changed the center of gravity in 1969.

What can I say about Milton Hall except that it was the only source of food within a mile of campus. Zoning restrictions prohibited commercial buildings within a mile of campus. There was no Pan Am Center and the closest convenience store was on Espina Street with another a little farther away on Solano Drive. Neither were there soft drink or snack machines located anywhere on campus. There were, however, water fountains in every building.

The cafeteria dominated the entire south end of the main floor of Milton, and Irene was happy to work there, since both of us had to scrape to make ends meet at a time when tuition might have been $200, but student jobs were scarce, and we were like most students who depended upon the meal card purchased at registration time to make sure we had three meals a day. No, the food was not any better then than I hear it is in Taos Cafeteria in Corbett Center 50 years later.

Some things probably do not change. The football team was close knit during my days at NMSU. They lived together in the dorms and they ate together in the cafeteria, which went a long way to building team solidarity. As I remember, the players on the 1960 team were held to a high academic standard as well. Coach Woodson insisted that they attend classes and maintain a good grade point average.

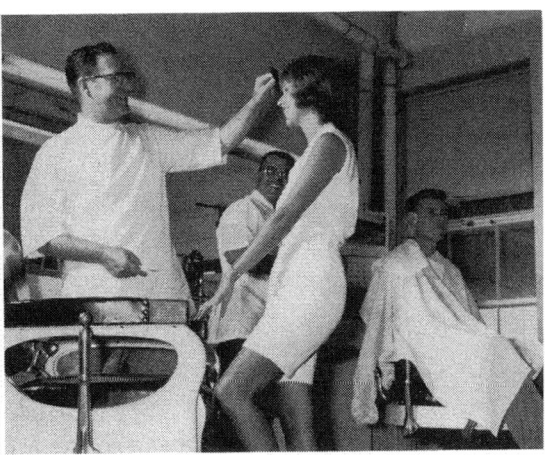

The Milton Student Center housed a bookstore, cafeteria, student offices, newspaper, yearbook, a barber shop and a downstairs bowling alley. Upstairs was a ballroom. (NMSU Yearbook photo)

During the Woodson years that I remember, players generally made it to graduation. They were as serious about their academics as they were about their football. Some of that rubbed off on me as a journalism major and reporter, and I made it in four years as well.

Milton Hall was always bustling. Not only was there a cafeteria, but the building housed student government and all its activity offices. The NMSU yearbook *Swastika* had its office, *The Round Up* was at the bottom of the west stairway, right beside the barbershop, and down the other side of that stairway was the student bookstore. The entire north part of the main floor was the ballroom. Above the main portal was painted the reminder "The Days That Make Us Happy Make Us Wise." Down the stairs from the cafeteria was called the "sub," with its bowling alley, pinball machines and other amenities suitable for a student activities center.

Walking out the east doors of Milton it was an easy walk to my dormitory room in Breland. Garcia Hall was another men's dormitory up the hill. Just south of Milton was the Women's Residence Center.

An aerial view showing Breland and Garcia men's dormitories and the Milton Student Center, with desert south and east of the buildings. (NMSU Yearbook photo)

Women rarely lived off campus, and life in the WRC was carefully regulated. Men could visit the lobby of the WRC but never the individual rooms. Irene lived in WRC, and I remember clearly that the curfew for lobby visitors was 9:30, and the girls had to be safely cloistered after that time. The rules were relaxed on the weekends, but it was still annoying to those guys fortunate enough to have a girlfriend – I say that because there were always five men to every woman attending NMSU in those days.

What about us guys? Well, male students were not restricted. We could be out walking or going from place to place 24 hours a day. Fat lot of good that did us! After all, few of us had cars and we had very little spending money. On a rare night, we might walk all the way past old Hiram Hadley's two-story house and on to where University Avenue now meets Valley Drive, and where there was a drive-in restaurant.

Some people may be surprised to learn that the parking lot where Jordan Street enters the campus past the WRC was not paved, because Milton Hall was close to being the end of the world. As a matter of fact, going out on Jordan and turning right on University, the pedestrian would pass the ZTA house and the DZ house only to find that the University Avenue pavement ended at Locust Street, and the dirt road went directly out into the desert past A Mountain.

One of the most unusual features of the NMSU campus in 1960 was a number of WWII wooden barracks moved to campus by President Roger B. Corbett as he pressured the New Mexico Legislature for capital funds to build living space for the growing student population. I never had to live in the White Rock barracks, but many male students arriving in the summer of 1960 spent at least one semester bunking in the wartime quarters probably moved to the campus from Ft. Bliss in El Paso.

A map of Las Cruces in Branson Library shows that Las Cruces came to an end at the Locust-University intersection, and there was no development in Las Cruces south of University.

In remembering the community before the era of the Interstates, U.S. Highway 180 came through Las Cruces from Arizona, right through Main Street in town and south to El Paso. Some people have forgotten, but Main Street in Las Cruces ended at the intersection of Idaho Street where it becomes Avenida de Mesilla. At that point, it became Maple Drive, going south into Mesilla Park. There were a couple of motels on Maple Drive, and even a hotel across from the Mesilla Park Station of the AT&SF Railway, but the latter I only knew about from talking with long-time residents.

While University Avenue went straight west to Mesilla Park, the traditional homes of university faculty members were concentrated south of the irrigation ditch while chile and cotton fields dominated the land north of University. Actually, College Avenue was very much the main route taken by faculty to and from the campus.

That all came to an end when Interstate 10 changed the landscape. Of course I also remember that El Paseo Drive, where Las Cruces High School was located, turned into Union Avenue that also looped south and west into Mesilla Park, acoss Maple Drive and past the suburb where Prof. Clyde Tombaugh lived and across Highway 28 and on to the river. Ah yes, where the Drinkin' Tree waited for us! I think I already mentioned that.

Mesilla Park had a Texaco station, the hotel I mentioned, grocery stores, and even a movie theater that I think I visited at least once. These places were close enough to walk to, but I don't remember students making too much use of those facilities; they were there for Mesilla Park residents and for travelers who arrived at the railway depot.

So where did we go to shop in the days before shopping malls? Well, downtown of course. A bus ran regularly from campus down Solano Drive, west on Lohman Avenue at the intersection of where the new Cork 'n' Bottle restaurant served Las Cruces as well as being a popular watering hole for the adult student body. Proceeding down Lohman, the bus passed the Las Cruces Police Department on the north side of Lohman and thence to Main Street where a full array of shops were open from Chance's Newsstand to Sonny Klein's furniture store, the gun store, the Rio Grande and State theaters, Jay Druxman's men's apparel, the Rexall Drug store, Popular Dry Goods, Anthony's (a good place to buy cheap underwear), and a drive-in restaurant at the intersection of Main and Lohman. Amador studios, the leading photographic studio in Las Cruces at that time, was located downtown.

Of course there were a couple of bars downtown, including the famous Welcome Inn that always had a devoted clientele and was always visited regularly by the cops, especially on the weekend.

Downtown was dominated by the peaceful Catholic church that offered an air of dignity to the city and extended east to west from Church Street to Main. The main Las Cruces post office was on Church, which ran parallel to Main, as was the major teen hangout, The Shamrock Drive-in. Across the street south of the post office was *The Las Cruces Citizen*, the city's weekly newspaper.

On the other side of Main Street, running parallel to Main, was Water Street. I knew that street well because it was the home of the *Las Cruces Sun-News* at the intersection of Water and Griggs streets. That's where I would visit sports editor Abe Perilman. Orville Priestley and his sons owned both newspapers in Las Cruces in those days.

More importantly, next to the newspaper office was a small kiosk housing Day's Hamburgers, a traditional lunch choice for Las Crucens in general and newspaper staffers in particular since the 1930s. Thank goodness they were still in business 50 years later, within 100 yards and in sight of their old location, in a recent building now occupied by the offices of the El Paso Electric Company. The Sun-News also moved, but just went along Griggs to the old Safeway grocery store location at the intersection of Griggs and Alameda.

After 1965 with the completion of the Interstate, I heard that Las Cruces closed Main Street downtown and converted it into a mall. That experiment ended in 2011, and I hear that traffic is again moving along Main Street as it did in 1960.

The history of Las Cruces was similar to that of Roswell in that the populations of both cities were beneficiaries of the presence of a military base. Roswell had Walker Air Force Base and Las Cruces had White Sands Missile Range.

Roswell was actually larger than Las Cruces in 1960, when Las Cruces listed 29,000 citizens and Roswell 39,000. The closure of Roswell's air force base in 1967 resulted in a population drop, while Las Cruces kept growing. Today, Roswell's population is 48,000, while Las Cruces has reached 100,000. The presence of WSMR has no doubt been a constant stimulus for Las Cruces, although New Mexico State University has also been instrumental in spurring community growth.

– Dan Perry 2012

CHAPTER ONE
In the Beginning — 1894-1928

The New Mexico College of Agriculture and Mechanic Arts, Las Cruces, in the late 1800s. (Courtesy of New Mexico State University Archives and Special Collections Department)

 New Mexico State University's first recognized football game – "foot-ball" in those days – was played in 1894 when the school was New Mexico College of Agriculture and Mechanic Arts. New Mexico was still a territory. It would not become a state, the 47th, until 1912. W.M. Clute is identified as the Aggie coach and captain as well as the right half back. This makes him not only the first Aggies coach but also the first of four Aggies to coach their alma mater.

 For the nitpickers, it is not known why foot-ball had a hyphen and half back was sans the little dash. Perhaps it was just a dash of undergraduate journalism. It all began for New Mexico State with a one-game season, an 18-6 loss in Albuquerque at the University of New Mexico. There are repeated mentions over the years that this was the first intercollegiate football game in New Mexico, marking the start of the intrastate rivalry.

In an early indication New Mexico State and the University of New Mexico are separated by more than 225 miles on Interstate, UNM claims the first football game between the two schools was a year earlier, in 1883, in Albuquerque, a 25-5 New Mexico win.

We'll stick with the account in the *New Mexico Collegian*, at that time the New Mexico A&M student newspaper, which goes with 1894.

This said, there is in existence a photograph of 16 apparently extremely fit young men identified as being members of the 1893 football team. If the year is correct, an assumption, and that's all we can do at this point, is since an Aggie Athletic Association was organized in 1893, this team was not an officially sanctioned team. Rather, it was what now would be classified a club team. So if there indeed was a game that year, it was between standard issue undergraduates as well as students who had lingered on campus for five or more years as well as some healthy fellows from town, all having a little head-knocking fun.

One point on which the schools agree is they did not play again until the next century, in 1905, when New Mexico State won, 40-0, in Las Cruces.

A Prof. Hagerty is quoted about the earlier game in the January 1894 edition of *New Mexico Collegian*. The good professor's cryptic remarks make it clear second-guessing and football are old accomplices.

Prof. Hagerty said, "I think there are four reasons for our defeat. First, the boys were not defeated by the University. They were beaten by the University and the town together. Second, Captain Clute seemed to have his day off, and made several pretty bad plays, probably because he could have played better at full back than half back. Third, the full back had practiced only one day for his position which was not enough by any means. Fourth, if Joseph Bennett had practiced with the team, and played as half back, in all probability the boys would have won the game against the 'combination.' "

"The town" no doubt refers to members of the UNM team who were not students. This was not a suggestion NCAA rules were violated. The NCAA had yet to be formed to tilt at windmills. In the early years of college football, it was not unusual for a team to bolster its lineup with graduate students or even non-students. Clute himself appears to have played for the Aggies for more than the standard four undergraduate years.

The Agricultural College of New Mexico, as it referred to itself, was, in the words of college president Hiram Hadley in a full-page statement printed in the same January 1894 edition of the *New Mexico Collegian*, "… the Best Equipped Educational Institution in New Mexico. It offers choice of four courses. 1. Agriculture; 2. Mechanical Engineering; 3. Civil Engineering; 4. Ladies' Course.

"The equipment of the College consists of a fine three-story brick and stone building, mechanical shops, chemical and other laboratories, a library of over two thousand volumes, an extensive list of magazines, and over ten thousand dollars' worth of physiological, entomological, botanical, chemical and mechanical apparatus and machinery. Practical and Thorough training is given in all departments.

"A first-class Preparatory School is sustained to prepare students for entrance to the College proper.

"Expenses: Tuition is free and text-books are loaned to students or sold at actual cost, but an annual enrollment, or entrance fee of $3.00 is charged each student; also, each student must make a deposit of $5.00 as security for any damage done to property or to pay for books damaged or lost. This will be returned when the student withdraws, if there are no charges against it. Good board and lodging can be secured at from $16 to $20 per month within walking distance of the College."

Shifting back to extracurricular activities, the December 1893 *New Mexico Collegian*, mentions "W.M. Clute, of Lansing, Mich. is coaching the foot ball team."

We have no explanation for the absence of a hyphen here beyond student journalist lack of consistency.

From an article in the January 1894 *New Mexico Collegian*, we learn that "Although foot-ball is in its infancy in New Mexico, the first inter-collegiate contest taking place on New Year's Day, there are already objections to the game offered, almost without exception by those people who have formed their opinions by the comments of a sensational press, and the ridicule of comic magazines."

Back when concussions were shrugged off

This was a double-edged attack, blaming the ills of the world on the press along with mention of the debate about the dangers inherent in young men hurtling themselves against one another. Questions about the dangers that come with playing football continue today. Once upon a time, concussions were shrugged off as merely "ringing your bell." There is no more shrugging, not with hard evidence from documentation of what happens when players are concussed.

The article, clearly a heartfelt defense of the sport, continued: "The public rules, indirectly, all athletics; athletics also, in a college town, largely rule the public in the gratification of their sporting instincts. It is to the interest of both factions to agree on athletic questions. That foot-ball games draw large crowds by catering to the people's brutal instincts is a very mistaken idea. What the people disapprove of is carefully remedied by the foot-ball authorities, as the frequent modifying of rules, and prohibition of dangerous plays bear witness. The playing rules are also changed by the authorities when, in their opinion, such changes will tend to elevate the game; and many alterations have been made before the general public has become aware of existing evils.

"Without doubt, foot-ball possesses more attraction for the spectator, and is the most beneficial game for the participants in America. In its movements, there is required of every player the greatest physical strength and endurance, activity, a cool head, and keen perception. The game calls forth all the abilities of head and body. Every play is carefully planned. The spectators see, perhaps, a wedge, a rush, a heavy mass of players, a heap of fallen bodies; but eleven men in that instant of play were devoting their entire energy to the accomplishing of a certain definite move. Perhaps you see a half back running with the ball. He is, to the average spectator doing all the playing. Yet ten players are assisting him every moment he is moving, each one holding a position assigned him that particular movement. So it is all through the game – a game of team work, of concerted action, of strength, of skill and strategy.

"The principal points objected to in the game at present are momentum plays, inaugurated in '91 and which have reached their highest development the past season. These plays will probably be prohibited by the Board of Control at their next meeting, and various others, changes will be made to lessen the apprehensions of timid spectators. As the game is played today, the dangers and accidents are wonderfully exaggerated."

The article is signed by none other than W.M. Clute. His passionate plea for the public to understand that the authorities are vigilant in their quest to make the game safe has been heard by others repeatedly over the years. It is heard today from NCAA president Mark Emmert and NFL commissioner Roger Goodell.

Eminent New Mexico State University historian Walter Hines, who has chronicled Aggie history on bleedCRIMSON.net, set the scene when he wrote, "… the Aggies were a rough and spirited bunch. The pre-1920s were the days of no helmets, little padding, and few passes. Under the tutelage of unpaid faculty members who doubled as coaches, the Aggies had a sparkling winning record of 32-18-7 from 1894 to 1910. The two best-known early coaches were William Sutherland, identified in *The Round Up* as an 1898 New Mexico A&M graduate, and the indomitable John O. Miller, a Colorado University graduate, who also served the college as registrar. These men were followed by a succession of fine coaches like pioneer coach Amos Alonzo Stagg protege Arthur Badenoch of the University of Chicago and Robert 'Cap' Brown of Dartmouth. From 1911 to 1928, with football shutdown in 1918 due to World War I, the Aggie footballers were 76-37-6, including a 8-7-2 record against their big brothers from UNM."

Labeling UNM "big brother" is interesting considering it was founded in 1889, one year after New Mexico State was established. The comment reflects UNM being located in Albuquerque, which has a much larger population, therefore greater political clout, than New Mexico State in Las Cruces.

Think for a moment about Miller as registrar-coach. There is reason to put registrar first because there is no doubt that assignment took up the bulk of his time. History tells us many coaches of this era were professors volunteering their spare time or graduate students doing likewise. Can you imagine the look on the face of Alabama's Nick Saban, with a salary listed at $7.16 million a season, if the head of campus human resources told him henceforth he would be paid a professor's salary, teach a full load of classes and coach the football team for the love of the game?

Here's a footnote for the economists: A season ticket in 1911 was $3 for students and $5 for others.

Hines also wrote about the "pigskin" or football, which was not the sleek ball ued today. Instead, it "was large and round, requiring an odd flat-handed passing motion." It was similar to a rugby ball, better suited for kicking in an era when the drop-kick was in vogue. They played a "plodding" game, Hines wrote, in which "strategy dictated punting on third down inside your own 40-yard line, and 18-20 punts a game were the norm."

Manning and Brees would not favor this football

The Aggies play El Paso in 1907. (Courtesy of New Mexico State University Archives and Special Collections Department)

A photograph of Miller's 3-0 1907 team includes 13 players and Miller. The player in the center of the group is holding one of those large, round pigskins. Show the photo to Payton Manning or Drew Brees and all either would do is groan.

Miller is in a suit wearing a white dress shirt with a high collar and a bow tie. No hoodie. No t-shirt. No logos promoting a team or a clothing company. It was a formal time, even where football was concerned.

In June 1894, the *New Mexico Collegian* refers to another game, this one a win against Las Cruces. There is no other reference to this game, and it is not enshrined in the NM State *2014 Football Media Guide*. In the same article, we are told "O.C. Snow, their manager and center-rush is due the most honor in the success of the team. By his untiring efforts, they have been enabled to fit up a good ground upon the campus and to purchase the suits, shin-guards, nose protectors, banner, and other paraphernalia with which they are equipped." The story is signed by "One of Team." There is a photo of the members of the 1894 team, 16 strong, W. Clute, coach, and O.C. Snow, '94, Capt., Center.

Clute's name pops up again in the *New Mexico Collegian* December 1895 edition as "again coaching the College foot ball team." The *2014 Football Media Guide* lists Alfred Holt (no alma mater listed) as coach of the 2-0 1895 team with a 1-0 forfeit win over El Paso and a 10-4 win over El Paso High. We are told there was no coach in 1896 when the Aggies were 0-2, losing 10-0 to Fort Bliss and 6-0 to Las Cruces. There's a January 1896 report of a 22-0 win over Fort Bliss. Clute is the quarterback, identified in print as the Qr. Back. This was a "joint College and Las Cruces team" and is not recognized by NMSU.

Aiding and abetting the confusion from the early years, the *New Mexico Collegian,* this time the January 1899 edition, refers to two games in 1893 – College 10, Las Cruces 0 and College 6, Albuquerque 18. Fast forward to October 28, 1909 when the school newspaper now is *The Round Up*. We're back to square one with the following report: "The game with the University took place on January 1, 1894 at Albuquerque and was the first intercollegiate football game played in New Mexico." (Note the modern usage of football.) The January 1, 1894 date is repeated on November 11, 1913 and November 28, 1916.

Going forward, the Aggies enjoyed moderate success in relatively short seasons on the gridiron. Charles M. Barber (no alma mater listed) was 3-1-1 (1-0-1 and 2-1) in 1897-98, Miller was 1-0 in 1899, Sutherland was 3-3-1 in 1900, Miller returned from 1901 to 1907 to win 15 more games while losing four and tying four to post an overall 16-4-4 record, W.G. Hummel (Illinois) was 4-2 in 1908, J.H. Squires (Cornell) was 1-3-1 in 1909, Badenoch was 22-3-1 from 1910-1913 as schedules were expanded, Clarence W. Russell (Chicago) was 7-7-1 from 1914 to 1916 and John G. Griffith (Iowa) was 4-2 in 1917.

Miller was 10-0 over his last three seasons. Badenoch had a 12-game winning streak and closed his years with a 19-1-1 run. Until 1914, games against high schools were counted in the official records of a coach. Starting in 1915, some of those games became exhibitions, more like pre-season scrimmages today, and were not part of the coach's record. But some high school games counted as late as 1925. Russell's only losing season – winless in four games – came in 1916. There had to be some disruption that year with Pancho Villa crossing the border from Mexico to raid Columbus, N.M. Deke Houlgate's *The Football Thesaurus* tells us "a New Mexico national guard co., composed almost entirely of Aggie students, was called for border duty."

Life on campus obviously was impacted by the war, as you can tell from following in an October 24, 1917 story in *The Round Up*: "Immediately after assembly of last week the Senior class held a meeting for the purpose of organization. It was not an imposing gathering as far as numbers go, as only five of last year's Junior class returned this year.

However, there is reason for this. Besides the number who found for one reason and another that they could not get their degrees this year, no less than six of the class of '18 are now either members of Uncle Sam's khaki-clad army or are helping to raise more crops with such to feed that army."

Charles Cormany was elected class president, W.P. Sinnock vice president, Miss Margaret Buvens secretary and Miss Dette Rentfrow treasurer. What about senior class member No. 5? That was Chester Garrett who "while not holding office this year, is very prominent factor in both class and college affairs. He is an Ag. Man specializing in dairying and has done some splendid work in his line.

"The class of 1918, while probably the smallest Senior class that the college has had for some time, is out to demonstrate this year that quality counts for more than quantity."

Continuing with the coaches, the *Football Media Guide* tells us Anthony Savage (Washington) was 2-3-1 in 1919, Arthur J. (Dutch) Bergman (Notre Dame) was 12-5-1 from 1920 to 1922, Robert (Cap) Brown (Dartmouth) was 20-6-1 in 1923-25, Arthur R. Burkholder (Kansas Agricultural College, now Kansas State) was 5-3-1 in 1926 and Ted R. Coffman (USC) was 7-10 in 1927-28. Miller, with eight years, was the longest serving coach from 1894 to 1928. Badenoch was next in the longevity line with his four-year stretch.

Lost in the mist of time

As tends to be the case with old records, there is some disagreement about who coached when during New Mexico State University's early football years.

The official NMSU list supplied by the *Football Media Guide* begins as follows: 1894 W.M. Clute, 1895 Alfred Holt, 1896 no coach, 1897-98 Charles M. Barber, 1899 John O. Miller, 1900 William Sutherland, 1901-07 Miller again, 1908 W.G. Hummel, 1909 J.H. Squires, 1910-13 Arthur H. Badenoch, 1914-16 Clarence W. Russell, 1917 John G. Griffith, 1918 no team, 1919 Antony Savage, 1920-22 Arthur J. Bergman, 1923-25 Robert Brown, 1926 Arthur R. Burkholder and 1927-28 Ted R. Coffman.

Cursory research by historian Hines for a slideshow a number of years ago turned up 1899-1907 Miller, no coaches for 1908 and 1909, 1910-13 Badenoch, 1914-16 Russell, 1917 Griffith, 1918 no football, 1919 Savage, 1920-22 Bergman, 1923-26 Brown, and 1927-28 Coffman.

What are you going to do, tape the names of the coaches to a wall, close your eyes, throw darts at them and go with the names the darts hit to settle this?

You can research the *Collegian*, *The Round Up* and *Swastika* and see what you find. The yearbook indicates Bergman was the coach in 1922 with Brown, identified variously as R.R. and Cap, at the helm in 1923-24-25.

"In the earliest years, I saw a couple of accounts where the teams practiced without a coach until the day of a game?" Hines wrote in an email.

The question mark clearly was shorthand for "can you believe that?" Indeed you can. This was an era when football truly was a student activity.

"I knew Sutherland coached for one year during the Miller tenure, but I am also thinking that Miller was the real coach who asked Sutherland for help due to Miller's other duties as registrar and professor," Hines wrote.

His suggestion basically comes down to going with NMSU records when in doubt.

A footnote about the yearbook is provided by Hines when talking about his father serving in World War II with the 120th Combat Engineers in the 45th Division, comprised of men from New Mexico, Oklahoma and Texas.

"There were Indians in the unit," he said in an interview. "Their arm patch started out as a *Swastika*, which is a Navajo symbol. It was changed to the Thunderbird."

The obvious reason for the change was, of course, the enemy in World War II was Hitler's Third Reich, which used the *Swastika* as its primary symbol. The 1925 yearbook, long before WWII, traces the *Swastika* to the Sanskrit language, to ancient Egyptian records as well as to the Pima and Navajo Indians.

Back to who coached when. There is no evidence beyond the *Football Media Guide* that Sutherland, listed in the guide as a New Mexico State graduate and as the coach in 1900, actually was the coach. He is mentioned as the "Full Back" on the team that season in the *New Mexico Collegian*. Demonstrating his versatility, he also was the "Athletic" reporter for the Collegian. He would go on to earn a law degree at George Washington University in Washington, D.C., serve as secretary to future president William Taft when Taft was governor-general of the Philippines and eventually return to Las Cruces to practice law. A Sept. 19, 1916 story in *The Round Up* is typical. He is identified as "famous player while in college" in a story about a football assembly.

The Aggies could not reel in a coach after Miller packed it in until Hummel, an instructor, stepped up for a season. A year earlier, in a story about seniors defeating faculty, 21-1, in what was loosely labeled a baseball game, he played shortstop.
"Rumor says that Hummel was once a big-leaguer," the story reads. That's Hummel with one L. Immediately below the article are the lineups in which the faculty shortstop was Hummell with two Ls.

They could not get it straight in the same edition of the paper. *The Baseball Encyclopedia* makes it clear the tale about him playing in the majors was, like most rumors, false. The only Hummel or Hummell to play in the majors at that time was John E. Hummel, who played first base, second base, shortstop and outfield for the Dodgers from 1905 to 1917 and with the 1918 Yankees. He hit .241 in 1908. His career batting average was .254.

No one else named Hummel or Hummell is listed. *The Football Media Guide* identifies him as Hummell.

How do we determine Hummel over Hummell? The February 26, 1908 edition of *The Round Up* features a story about agricultural machinery written by W.G. Hummel. The assumption is Professor Hummel signed the article he presented to the newspaper and that he knew how to spell his own name. Also, a check of the electronic archive of *The Round Up* turns up Hummel 23 times in 1908 and 1909 to Hummell six times. So Hummel it is.

Next up on the coaching firing line for one painful season was Squires. Away from the football field, Coach Squires was agronomy professor Dr. Squires. Was he on the firing line or was he a target? His team opened the season with a scoreless tie against El Paso Military. Then came a 6-0 loss to Arizona and a 19-0 win against New Mexico Mines. At that point, the Aggies had outscored the opposition, 19-6. They should have quit when they were ahead. Along came New Mexico Military, a two-year college at that time, to humble the Aggies, 34-0. That was just a warm-up. They closed the season with "the worst defeat in college history," as *The Round Up* headline read of the 51-0 outcome at UNM. They were outscored 85-0 in those two games.

Griffith prompted a yearbook writer to wax poetically as follows: "When a coach is able to enter a place for the first time, take charge of a string of green men, none of whom he has ever seen before, and turn out a team able to hold its own against many other teams of experienced players, and to defeat an old rival 110 to 3, he can proclaim his title anywhere without fear of contradiction. In a few words, that is what Coach J.G. Griffith did last year in football. With four old men back, he molded a team that scored 235 points against the opponents' 75."

The old rival was the University of New Mexico. The assumption is "old men" refers to returning lettermen.

The tribute continued: "Most of his success is due to his wonderful personality, imbuing his pep and enthusiasm into his teams, making them fight to the last ditch and never giving up. In basketball he trained the team which won the state championship by their fast and aggressive work. In baseball, with hardly any material, a promising bunch for next year is in sight.

"With sixteen years of valuable experience in coaching behind him, from '02 to '07 with Idaho, from '07 to '10 in Iowa, from '10 to '15 at Idaho again, from '15 to '17 with Oklahoma, and from '17 to –, with the New Mexico Aggies, who can tell what next year has in store for the Aggies? It may be said with confidence, however, that in the race for the southwestern championship next year, the Aggies will not be far from the top."

Mention of the southwestern championship and subsequent mention of players winning all-southwestern honors is a generic term not to be confused with the Southwest Conference, which reigned supreme in this corner of the country from 1914 to 1996. And, instead of racing toward a mythical football championship, the Aggies moth-balled their football team in 1918 as they faced the realities of WWI. Then, in 1919, Savage took over as their coach.

Xs and Os and Biology

You cannot help but notice the frequency in which Griffith changed jobs. A March 15, 1921 story in *The Round Up* has him winning a basketball championship at Pasadena High out in California. This story reports he coached the Aggies for three years and taught biology for two years.

Those assignments apparently overlapped. He was the acting Head of the Biology Department in 1918. At one time, late in '18, he spent several weeks at Princeton "taking a special course in Athletics," according to *The Round Up*. In 1920, identified as Professor Griffith, he was voted the most popular faculty member by students, receiving 220 votes to 52 for Miss Winningham and 43 for Miss Armitage.

Arthur Bergman was "Dutch" Bergman, or "Little Dutch." He had an older brother, Alfred, "Big Dutch," a former Notre Dame star. Alfred, who was 5-foot-8, 160 pounds, was right halfback for the Irish in 1910 and the quarterback in 1911-1913-1914. Arthur, 5-8, 149, a roommate of fabled Notre Dame star George Gipp, was a right halfback there in 1915-1916-1919. He played for Knute Rockne in '19. A third brother, Joe, was a backup Notre Dame left halfback in 1921-1922-1923.

Arthur Bergman also coached at The Catholic University, where he was 59-31-4, from 1930 to 1940, plus he was coach of the Washington Redskins in the NFL in 1943.

Robert Rosewell (Cap) Brown came to New Mexico State from New Mexico Military Institute. There is a photo of him in the 1925 yearbook looking stylish. He's wearing an Ascot or newsboy cap, bow tie, jacket and knickers. The campus newspaper as well as the yearbook refer to his players as the "Fighting Farmers" and the team "The Fighting Farmer Squad." One of his stars was four-year letterman Jerry Hines, the father of Walter Hines. An "Our Coach" article in the yearbook points out that "Brown is not a new man in this part of the country, as he spent several years at N.M.M.I., where he coached many winning teams for the Cadets. His teams have humbled the Aggies, but it is to be hoped that will not happen again…"

Brown was a 1901 Dartmouth graduate said to have been an All-American as an undergraduate. Like the rumor about Hummel playing major league baseball, there is no evidence to support this story. The All-American team for 1900, which would have been his senior season, did include a Brown, only it was Yale's Gordon Brown, a Hall of Fame guard. Cap Brown coached at Virginia Tech, interestingly as head coach for a year before serving as assistant the following year, as well as at North Carolina, Washington and Lee, and Tulane before heading west to New Mexico Military. He returned to Rosewell and once again coached NMMI football after his time in Las Cruces. The best of his three years with the Aggies was his first, when the team was 8-0. He was praised by *The Round Up* for accomplishments beyond football because "he has built up girls athletics to a point heretofore unknown in the history of State College."

Women athletes were called girls back then. Can you imagine the reaction of the UConn women's basketball or U.S. national women's soccer teams if someone referred to them as girls? At least things were balanced. The men who played football early in the 1900s frequently were called boys. It was just a sign of the times.

Burkholder slipped in to coach the 1926 team. Known as A.L. and Bill, he taught in the Animal Husbandry Department and was advance manager in 1922 when the Aggies traveled to San Francisco to play St. Mary's. For some unknown reason, the *Football Media Guide* has the Aggies playing St. Mary's Indian School. *The Round Up* clearly states the game was against St. Mary's College. The Swastika refers to the game against St. Mary's College of Oakland at Recreation Park in San Francisco. St. Mary's was located in Oakland before moving in 1928 to Moraga.

Adding to the picture of what it was like in the 1920s, the Aggies were gone from campus almost two weeks because their next game was in Tucson against Arizona. After playing St. Mary's, they traveled to Los Angeles, where they spent the week practicing, including scrimmaging against USC. They did not arrive in Tucson until Friday.

Yet another how-it-was-then entry is found in the lineups for the 1926 Aggies-Institute (New Mexico Military) game. Hines is the Aggie quarterback. The entry in question is immediately below the lineups. Included are the game officials. Burkholder was the referee and Sutherland the timekeeper. At a later date, Burkholder is called "the best referee in the southwest." How interesting if Burkholder was working with William A. Sutherland 26 years after he perhaps coached the Aggies.

There's more local color. The December 1, 1925 edition of *The Round Up* refers to New Mexico Military as the "Roswell Cadets." The 19-0 victory by the Aggies is hailed with this excited headline: "The Farmer Machine Worked Perfectly." Yet another substitute nickname for the Aggies was "Collegians."

Burkholder's fulltime assignments on campus were as a special instructor for Vocational Board men, on project work with those students and as athletic director.

Long before social media people wrote letters. Here's an open letter from an Aggie parent to *The Round Up* in 1926:

"Dear Sir:

"I have been watching your games with a great deal of interest and there is one thing that I wish to call your attention to.

"In all the newspaper accounts of the games there is always the same notation, 'The Aggies played a CLEAN, FAST, HARD game.'

"I would rather see your team lose and have this said about them, than to see you roll up a big score and have the papers say, 'they were a dirty bunch of players.'

"When a team has done its very best it is no crime to lose, but crooked playing is a crime of the worst sort. I am proud of the fact that my boy is playing with such a fine bunch of fellows and in charge of a man who, by his every word and action, says 'play clean boys, even if you lose them all.'

"I am not the only one who has noticed this. Tell your boys for me, that the 'Old

Boys' are watching them and wishing them all kinds of success, both in play and work.

"I expect to see you play Thanksgiving."

Someone needed to show this letter to New England Patriots coach Bill Bilichick.

One area of agreement between the *Football Media Guide* and historian Walt Hines is that among the in-the-beginning Aggies football coaches, Miller, Badenoch, Russell, Griffith, Bergman, Brown, Coffman, Jerry Hines and Julius Johnston also coached basketball.

We're talking about the era in which there was no more important development than when players started wearing helmets. Not all the players were willing to protect their heads. Granted, the level of protection with the leather helmets of the time might have been minimal, but common sense dictates minimal was better than no protection.

This is the time of the 60-Minute Man. Leaving the field of play for anything short of a broken limb was considered a sign of weakness. When you see pictures of teams from these years, you see very few substitutes. So how, when and where did coaches develop the next wave of players? Whether reloading or rebuilding, where was the pipeline?

The Round Up answers the question. The Aggies had a team called, simply, the Second Team. This team would be called the junior varsity today. On the high school level, it might be the frosh-soph team, although it is not possible to be certain juniors and seniors did not play with the Seconds. They played Las Cruces High, El Paso High, various city teams and, presumably, other college Second teams.

One report, on November 30, 1911, when the campus newspaper identified the school as "Agricultural College, N.M.," carried the page one headline, "Second Team Wallops El Paso High School." The story: "The El Paso High School and the College second team met last Saturday in one of the fiercest football games of the year. The visitors were here to wipe out that ignominious defeat administered to them by the College first team three weeks ago. But in the meantime, the 'scrubs' had been making hay since their first defeat in El Paso." The prose leaves you scratching your head at least a little. What is known for sure is New Mexico State, aka the College Varsity, defeated El Paso High early in the month, 75-0. That's in the *Football Media Guide*. Eventually, the writer of this unsigned article will give these Aggies credit for a 17-6 victory. Reading stories of the time, it is not clear if the high school is playing starters, backups or even the junior varsity against the Seconds.

Some players would shift back and forth between Varsity and Second teams. On occasion, a player would play for both teams on the same day.

On November 6, 1917, this gushing praise appeared in *The Round U*p in the "About the Campus" column: "During the year the second team has received little mention in *The Round Up*. And we now wish to give them their due. Without a second team, no college football team can have life. We owe our victories to the second team. They are the main stay of the coach. They are always on the job, and it is in the second team that the coming football players are found. A second team is as necessary to a first team as air is to life.

"The second team has been out there working every night. They are willing to go up against a superior aggregation in order that that aggregation may bring victory to the school and they are making good. Many a practice scrimmage is harder to the first team than some of the real games."

Sounds like a college scout team of later years made up of transfers required to sit out a season, scholarship players buried deep on the depth chart and walkons who are practice fodder, out there without the benefit of scholarships simply because of their love of the game. OK, they do harbor hopes of making a favorable impression, getting into games and, best of all, receiving a scholarship, as was the case with free safety Davis Cazares, winner of NMSU's first Pervis Atkins Spirit Award in 2014.

CHAPTER TWO

In the Beginning — Hold on to Your Hat: 110-3

Payback is part of the package, Warren Woodson reportedly told a coach when that fellow grumbled he would get even for a whuppin' the Aggies under Woodson had just handed his team.

So it was with New Mexico State and the University of New Mexico.

UNM had not been a kind host in 1909 and 1916 when it won by identical 51-0 scores in Albuquerque. The Aggies did more than return the favor in one mighty blow in Las Cruces in 1917. As humbling as the 102 points allowed in two games was, how about losing, or winning, depending on which side of the fence you reside, by 107 points? That's what happened in '17 when the Aggies prevailed, 110-3.

Excitement on campus was palpable, as evidenced in a "FOOT BALL ISSUE" of *The Round Up* in which the ear (the small box next to the masthead at the top of page one) proclaimed, "AGGIES: WHOOPEE YEOW!" The all caps banner headline screamed, "AGGIES END THE SEASON WITH AN AVALANCHE OF POINTS." It was not until the smaller two-column headline immediately over the story that the student journalists got around to mentioning the 110-3 score.

The game was on Thanksgiving day. The Aggies got two drumsticks on that memorable day as the Seconds traveled about an hour west of Las Cruces to Deming, where they defeated Deming High, 20-0.

The Round Up had a backup nickname for Aggies, found in a bold face introduction to the game story, which reads, "Second Edition of Clod Hoppers Start to Follow in the Steps of the First Team."

A footnote to the big game of the day against the University of New Mexico is the lack of an actual nickname for the gentlemen from Albuquerque. The team was known as "The Varsity" or, by the simplified version, "Varsity." The now-familiar Lobos moniker did not come into being until the fall of 1920, at the suggestion of sophomore George S. Bryan, doing double duty as editor of the school newspaper, the U.N.M. Weekly, and as student manager of the football team. He wanted a livelier name for the newspaper. That it also became the nickname for the sports teams was a welcome bonus.

As for what can be loosely characterized as a game, as one-sided as it was, it did not come close to Georgia Tech's infamous 222-0 beat down of Cumberland College in 1916.

The final tally in Las Cruces was 16 touchdowns and 14 PATs for the Aggies. Foster, the captain, provided 7 touchdowns and all 14 PAT kicks for a grand total of

56 points. Ousterhout had 4 touchdowns, Lohman 2, and Robbins, Hedgcoxe and Harris each 1. Ousterhout is identified as the starting right tackle. Obviously, he had his own double duty assignment in the backfield.

UNM's lone score, a field goal in the third quarter, came on a drop kick, which has since been replaced by the place kick. Sports fans of today are likely to identify the drop kick with rugby rather than football. It was a standard part of football until 1934. That's when the shape of the ball, referred to as an "oval," was streamlined to improve passing, which in turn made it more difficult to drop the ball and kick it as it hit the ground, hence the term drop kick.

After one touchdown in this memorable game (for the Aggies at least), *The Round Up* reported, "To change their luck the (UNM) Varsity kicked off." Good luck with that.

The passing game was not something a quarterback today would recognize, a detail you realize when you read, "The Varsity unmuzzled a pass."

It was only three years earlier, in 1913, when Notre Dame stunned the football-following segment of the nation and, more specifically, Army, 35-13, by unveiling a passing attack — Gus Dorais to a pharmacy major named Knute Rockne. Young Mr. Rockne, seeing the potential of this game, would go on to make quite a name for himself as Notre Dame's football coach.

Football is not for the faint of heart. As they chronicled in *The Round Up*, "In the second quarter our spunky little quarter back, Vickers, tangled up with Clark, a man about twice his size. The referee said Vickers was to blame for the unpleasantness and banished him, at the same time penalizing the Aggies half the length of the field."

Elsewhere in *The Round Up*, John Griffith, the Aggies coach, is praised: "Our coach is right there with the goods, a driving, fighting man, capable of getting every ounce of energy out of the players that they have in them."

They certainly had plenty of energy against rival New Mexico on Thanksgiving Day in 1917.

CHAPTER THREE
In the Beginning — The Rentfrows

The reader today who peruses *The Round Up*, circa 1917, give or take a year or two, becomes something of an amateur anthropologist digging up information on football and beyond.

Just read the staff box of the newspaper in 1917. L.C. Campbell '19 is editor-in-chief and L.S. Ousterhout '19 is business manager. Among staff members covering beats ranging from athletics to society, along with agriculture and military, are Era Rentfrow, '19 household economics and Bendette Rentfrow, '18 Y.W.C.A.

Era Rentfrow served New Mexico A&M College and New Mexico State University 43 years, retiring as Registrar in 1962. This photo was taken in 1959. (NMSU Yearbook photo)

Miss Era Rentfrow is a symbol of a simpler, less complicated world before college athletic departments, as well as colleges themselves, developed a big business corporate culture. Born in 1898, she lived from an early age in nearby Mesilla Park. She attended and was president of Prep. Class, which apparently was an on-campus prep school. Bendette Rentfrow was her sister.

Miss Era Rentfrow's history is inexorably intertwined with the history of the university — one of 23 freshmen in 1915, graduate in 1919, university employee once she received her diploma, promoted to registrar in 1922, a position she held until retirement 40 years later in 1962. She was just finishing up her tenure as registrar when Warren Woodson's football team was placed on probation by the NCAA, the key charge being alleged admission irregularities.

Stories are told about Miss Rentfrow loaning money, her own money, to students short of cash for tuition, board or books. Legend has it none of those students were deadbeats. Each repaid her. Another story involves her telling a young man, when he registered, that his birth certificate made it clear his first name was Garrey, not Gary as he had spelled it on a form. The young man in question was Garrey Carruthers. His career path took him to become dean of NMSU's College of Business, governor of New Mexico and current NMSU President.

There's more. Joe Quesenberry, a three-time All-Southwestern tackle and two-time captain of the football team, was Miss Rentfrow's fiancé. Tragically, along came World War I. U.S. Army Capt. Quesenberry, an acting major in line for a permanent promotion, was the first Aggie killed in action, on April 29, 1918 on the Western Front. In 1933, the newly-constructed football field was named in his honor. As an undergraduate, he was cited as "a favorite with his team-mates; an Aggie determined to play clean football under all conditions ... a leader of which the college may well be proud of in the years to come." The stadium was renamed Aggie Memorial Stadium in 1950 to honor all Aggies who served in war. The playing field remained Quesenberry Field. The current Memorial Stadium is elsewhere on campus. It opened on September 16, 1978 with a 35-32 win over the University of Texas El Paso. Memorial Tower, which was incorporated into the College of Health and Social Services building, is the only part of Quesenberry Field/Memorial Stadium that remains today.

One of Miss Rentfrow's many contributions on campus is a photo display she organized honoring the 126 Aggies who died as soldiers in World War II.

Another entry on the long Miss Rentfrow-did-this-for-the-school list is she even served as alumni editor for *The Round Up.*

Rentfrow Gymnasium is named in her honor. An endowed fund, the Era Rentfrow Emergency Loan fund, was created in her memory.

Longtime NMSU watchers will tell you they never knew there was a second Rentfrow much less possibly a third, a brother. Tracking them in *The Round Up* and elsewhere provides a glimpse of life on campus 100 years ago. Call it quaint, folksy or just plain quiet, if you will. It definitely was small-town America as the country headed into the Roaring '20s.

The first mention in *The Round Up* of another Rentfrow is on January 17, 1913 when readers are informed the new officers of the "Christian Endeavor society of Mesilla Park" include Dette Rentfrow, secretary.

The approach of *The Round Up* in those days also can be identified as folksy. There's a page one story about the "second annual banquet of the Atadida," a campus literary society.

The first paragraph of the story sets the theme of the event: "The success of the second annual banquet of the Atadida was due to the excellent 'team work' of the various committees and to the loyal support of every member of the society." Such salient information as "the table was decorated in potted ferns, and a festive note was given by decorations of lavender and gold, the society colors" was included. "Between courses several readings, songs and humorous stories were given." Included was Dette Rentfrow reading "*A Modern Woman.*" The story ended with this bit of investigative reporting: "The washing of the dishes played an important part of the amusement of the evening, 'all hands and the cook' joining in on this very important ending of all really successful 'eat feasts.'"

There also is mention of Dette Rentfrow taking part in a debate during a campus Lyceum. In 1915, Dette Rentfrow, '18, Y.W.C.A., shares the staff box with Joe Quesenberry, '18, military. The following year, she presented Shakespearean sonnets during an assembly. About the same time, Dette Rentfrow became Bendette

Rentfrow in *The Round Up* staff box, no doubt deciding it was time to show the student body a more mature side of herself. Then there was the time at an assembly when the "hour was closed with another musical number, a violin and a mandolin duet by Misses Era Rentfrow and Ester Stuart, accompanied on the piano by Miss Dette Rentfrow."

Dette Rentfrow would eventually become president of the Y.W.C.A. Association. When she was elected treasurer of the senior class, *The Round Up* gushed, "She is taking a Domestic Science course and can be trusted to expend the class money to the best advantages."

In basketball in 1916, she displayed her ability to play at both ends of the court. In a 22-2 inter-squad win, she scored eight points as a forward in the first half, "throwing goals with deadly accuracy," before moving to defense for the second half.

They were playing the archaic six-players-on-a-side women's version of basketball in which three forwards remained in the front court and three guards in the back court, the midcourt line providing an iron curtain of sorts limiting players to one half of the court..

In a game against Las Cruces High, the breathless report praises: "Miss Ruth Phelps and Miss Dette Rentfrow starred at forward and their work was above reproach. Their passing from time to time completely baffled the less experienced Cruces guards. Miss Era Rentfrow and Miss Robbins played guards during the first half and proved to be a strong pair, for the Cruces forwards were unable to secure a field basket."

Editors also found room to slip in a note about Quesenberry in 1916 when Alamogordo High defeated Las Cruces High, 19-6, in Alamogordo, informing readers he made the trip, a notch less than 70 miles, to serve as referee.

There's high society and there's campus society

There's a October 24, 1916 news flash about how "The Misses Hill, Rentfrow and Rea entertained the members of the sophomore class in the home of Miss Julia Hill Friday evening. The home was decorated with cryanthemums. The members who arrived early started the evening by singing some of the popular songs, Miss Dette Rentfrow playing the piano for the people who could sing and those who enjoyed the art of trying to sing."

No doubt that was chrysanthemums.

And: "About the middle of the evening chocolates were served by Misses Rentfrow, Hill and Rea." Sister Era also was present that evening.

Also found is a wedding announcement on December 5, 1916. Among those attending the wedding were "Mrs. Rentfrow; Misses Era and Dette Rentfrow and Doyle Rentfrow."

This is the first mention of Doyle, presumably their brother.

On September 6, 1916 comes another flash, in the "About the Campus" column, telling readers, "Miss Mildred Fulghum and Dette Rentfrow returned Sunday from Estes Park, Colorado, where they have been attending the Y.W.C.A. convention."

Sister Era was just as busy, playing a violin solo for the Atadida Literary Society, serving as president of the Home Economics Club, secretary-treasurer of her sophomore class, having her name pop up in the paper for attending various social events, including a gardening class and participating as entertainment for the Ladies' Aid Society of Mesilla Park. When Vernice Bowers replaced her as treasurer a year later, the following was in *The Round Up*: "The treasurer will not have to stand empty-handed as Era still has some of last year's finances left."

In 1935, faculty and staff participated in intramurals, at least in the tennis tournament, in singles and doubles. Miss Rentfrow made the singles finals, results of which have not been uncovered.

Following graduation, Miss Rentfrow remained involved with *The Round Up*, writing the "Alumni News" column as well as another column, "Fighting Aggies," about former students during World War II. As the war was winding down, she wrote "Aggies In and Out of Service." She also contributed as a reporter, writing about four women students, each a war widow, enrolled in the department of home economics.

Miss Rentfrow remained the campus social butterfly, one example of which was the bridge party she had at her home, news of which was in the "Society" column of *The Round Up*. In the same article, she was identified as the guest of Misses Vida Strong and Margaret O'Loughlin at a bridge party at which she was a winner.

When Dette Rentfrow married Marine Capt. Shaler Ladd in February of 1919, the paper called them "two of the most popular of former students of State College … Miss Era Rentfrow, a sister of the bride, was bride's maid." The story included pertinent news as "The bride and groom entered to the strains of Lohengrin's Wedding March played by Miss Ann Berrier." Also: "The bride wore a white crepe de chine dress and carried a shower bouquet of white roses. The bride's maid, Miss Era Rentfrow, wore a pea green silk dress. The groom wore his service uniform of winter field."

Continuing the small-town newspaper approach, the "Alumni News" column in September 19, 1928 reported: "Dette Rentfrow (Mrs. Shaler Ladd) Home Ec. '18, is paying 'Era' and her mother an extended visit while 'hubby' Shaler, '18, is in Nicaragua with others of the marines. Shaler was on the U.S. Maryland for some time and made some very high target practice records with the six inch guns during the last few months. Dette is accompanied by her two daughters, one six years old and the other eight."

The investigative report also included the fact that "refreshments of salad, sandwiches, chocolate, cake and mints were served by misses Alice Steward and Era Rentfrow. The bride cut the bride's cake with her husband's saber." There also was this on a more serious level: "When the United States entered the war, Captain Ladd entered the service and has been through some of the fiercest of fighting in France during his period of service in the Marine Corps."

It was not Clarence Wins Russell

Of Doyle Rentfrow, assumed to be the brother of Era and Dette for no better reason than it makes sense he would have been mentioned if he was from another Rentfrow clan, very little is known for certain beyond the fact that he was a letterman on Clarence W. Russell's 1916 team that was 2-4-1. The wins came against an Alumni team, 27-0, and El Paso High, 20-0. The tie, 7-7, was in a return match against El Paso High. Toss those games out, as the NCAA does, and the Aggies were 0-4 against college teams. Obviously, Russell's middle initial did not stand for wins.

The first mention of Doyle Rentfrow comes in the October 20, 1914 edition of *The Round Up* when he is listed as a corporal in Company B of the Cadet Battalion, one of two companies, the other being Company A with Joe Quesenberry as captain. Fred Quesenberry was 2nd Lieutenant in Company B. New Mexico State is a land grant college. The Morrill Act of 1862, which established land grant colleges, had a requirement the schools include courses on military tactics. Why no mention of ROTC in the Rentfrow story? Because it was not until 1916 that President Woodrow Wilson established the Army Reserve Officers Training Corps, thus ROTC, in the National Defense Act.

Rentfrow was awarded a football letter in 1916, apparently at the age of 20. That's apparently because the only possible information on him comes from a list of those buried at the Evergreen Cemetery in Carrizozo, Lincoln County, New Mexico. The list includes Doyle Rentfrow, born 1896, July 30, death September 6, 1949. It is hard to believe they are not one and the same Doyle Rentfrow. His first mention as a football player comes during the second week of practice for the 1915 season in a "Pigskin Chasers Have Begun Practice In Earnest" story with no shortage of boosterism.

"After the first week of practice, the football team shows great promise," it begins. "The workout this week consisted mostly of falling on the ball, running down on punts, tackling and signal practice."

According to *The Round Up*, the Aggies, led by Coach Russell, would open the season against the Bulldogs of Las Cruces High, prompting this declaration: "…the High School is due for a good drubbing in the first practice game of the year."

Rentfrow was "an old student," one of "several men who had not shown any intention of coming out before." He was listed as weighing 150 pounds.

The story closed with the following paragraph: "With such bright prospects for the 1915 Aggie team, the student body should get together and organize the rooting department and get behind the team and boost. The rooting has a whole lot to do with winning football games, and as such a large number of the games are to be played on the home grounds, it can be used to a greater advantage than ever before. The first step is to elect a real live yell leader and then get out and work with him."

There is no mention of a game against Las Cruces High in the *Football Media Guide.* Once again we are left to assume. In this case, the assumption is it was more of a scrimmage than a game. *The Football Media Guide* does include two games against El Paso High, a 6-3 loss and a 26-0 win. These game are listed as exhibitions and are not counted in the record for the season. The official games were a 33-0 win over Texas College of Mines, a 3-0 win over Arizona, a 17-7 win against New Mexico Military and a disheartening 13-0 loss to New Mexico. That's a 3-1 record, as they did a much better job of chasing the pigskin than they would in 1916. Can a measure of blame be directed at the yell leader and the student body for not providing a sufficient boost for the team?

A photo of the 1915 team includes all of 21 players. There's Doyle Rentfrow, "sub right half." Also there are left tackle Joe Quesenberry and left end Shaler Ladd.

Doyle made news in a classroom, as reported in *The Round Up* of February 1, 1916: "A large stove upset in the Ag. Building last Monday morning, as a result of Doyle Rentfrow trying to make it stand up on six legs. Luckily for all present the fire had died down, and the stove was set up again on four legs only."

In another demonstration of hard-hitting journalism, the "Around the Campus" column on September 19, 1916 reported, "Messrs. Robert Thaxton and Doyle Rentfrow were visitors at Elephant Butte dam Wednesday."

A 1916 report: "Doyle Rentfrow is a Sophomore. He plays at center and he used to think that he was rough before he went to Arizona. Doyle has been learning this game fast. He will be very effective next year."

Rentfrow became effective sooner than predicted, starting at center in '16. He provided one of the few highlights against New Mexico that winless season with an interception.

One last mention, in "Old Student News" on November, 13, 1918: "Doyle Rentfrow, one of our Aggie Students, has had his over-seas equipment issued to him and expects to be 'over there' soon." Fortunately, the fighting was over two days earlier, on November 11, an indication on how slow news traveled in those days. The formal end of the war did not take place until June 28, 1919 with the signing of the Treaty of Versailles.

CHAPTER FOUR
In the Beginning — The Hines Years 1928-1939

New Mexico State fans with long memories smile at mention of Gerald H. Hines. Think Bear Bryant turning programs around at Kentucky, Texas A&M and Alabama. Think Urban Meyer, Mr. Fixit at Bowling Green, Utah, Florida and Ohio State. In terms of how Aggie supporters rallied around a coach, think Notre Dame's legendary Knute Rockne.

Jerry Hines, a native of neighboring Mesilla, Old Mesilla to locals, and a graduate of Las Cruces High, was a four-year letterman in both football and basketball at New Mexico A&M, as it then was called. He was a star end, halfback and quarterback as well as captain of the football and basketball teams. The football team was 25-8-1 (5-2, 8-0, 7-3, 5-3-1) and the basketball team was 48-31 (14-6, 10-9, 11-9, 13-7) during his undergraduate years. He graduated in 1926, and became football and basketball coach at Las Cruces High. He stepped up to become the Aggies football and basketball coach in 1929, and in 1930 added the duties of athletic director.

Beloved Aggie Head Coach Jerry Hines, in his time compared to Knute Rockne. (Courtesy of New Mexico State University Archives and Special Collections Department)

The Border Conference, officially the Border Intercollegiate Athletic Association, was formed in 1931 with New Mexico A&M, the University of New Mexico, Arizona, Arizona State Teachers-Tempe (now Arizona State University) and Arizona State Teachers-Flagstaff (now Northern Arizona University) as charter members. Arizona State-Tempe was known as the Bulldogs. It would not be until November of 1946 that Bulldogs was dropped in favor of Sun Devils.

Hines' early teams were up and down, going 3-2-3, 5-3, 6-4, 4-5-1 and 2-6, which gave him a middle-of-the-road 20-20-4 record during his first five years.

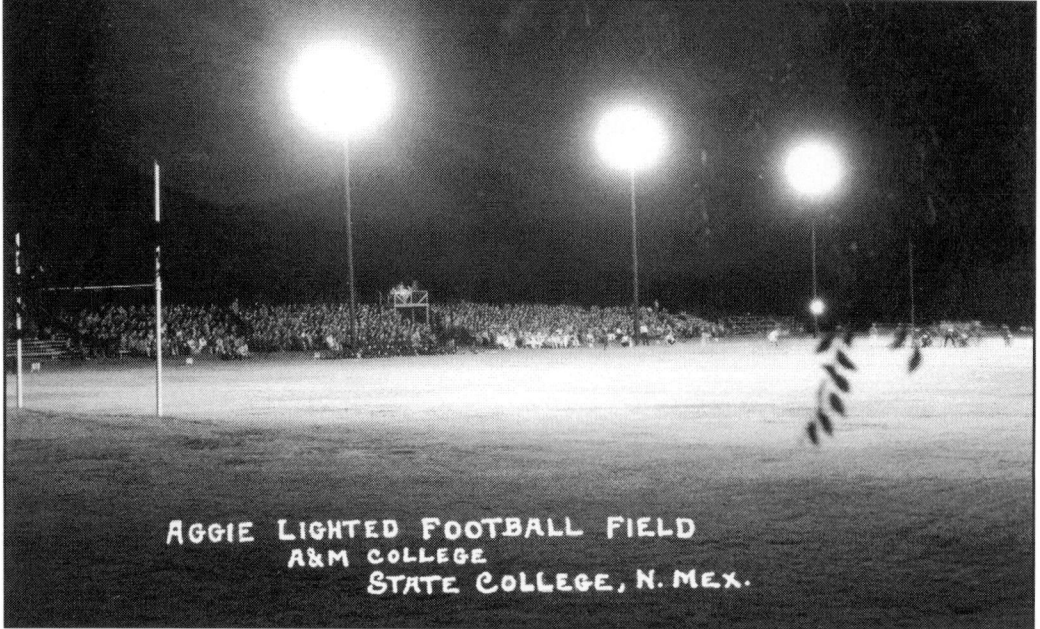

Night games were a novelty in the early years. This photo shows Quesenberry Field, later renamed Aggie Memorial Stadium. (Courtesy of New Mexico State University Archives and Special Collections Department)

Then came a perplexing 4-1-3 season in 1934. Was this a signal the Aggies were so very close to turning the proverbial corner? Or did they not want to see what was around the corner because the three ties were just a tease? It turned out to be a good omen. Hines led the Aggies to 7-1-2, 6-4-1, 7-2 and 7-2 records, 27-9-3 overall in 1935-36-37-38. This was a fine coach in his prime. Not only was this the best four-year record of the first 15 coaches in school history, only three coaches had lasted four or more years, which again speaks to the lack of continuity, stability and lack of continuing success of the football program pre-Hines.

The highlight of 1935 was playing in the inaugural Sun Bowl against Hardin-Simmons. Those Aggies had shut out their opponents five times. The Sun Bowl was a 14-14 tie. The 14 points by Hardin-Simmons were the most scored in a game against the Aggies. Included in the seven victories was an extremely satisfying 7-6 win against Arizona State. The scoring tally for the season was 210 points by the offense and 42 points for the opposition, providing an average of 21 points a game on offense against 4.2 points by the bad guys. The Aggies were a commendable 4-1 in the Border Conference. Arizona, identified as the "mighty Blue Brigade" by Kearney Egerton in his "Sideline Shots" column in *The Round Up*, was the champion with a 4-0 record.

Well, maybe that should be there were twin highlights, the first coming against rival UNM, which was cruising with a 6-1 record when along came New Mexico State. That lone Lobos loss was 25-0 at Oklahoma. They had not allowed a score in their six wins. That all changed against the Aggies, who, in Walter Hines' account, "thrashed" them, 32-0.

The success of the 1935 team apparently led to the installation of lights at Quesenberry Field. Walter Hines, in his opus on Aggies football, wrote, "huge crowds of more than 5,000 fans were becoming commonplace in Las Cruces.

The lowlight of the season quite obviously was the first tie, a great big double goose egg score versus New Mexico Western, then called Silver City Teachers College. What had to be frustrating about that 0-0 game was the fact that this was a season in which Western lost by identical 46-0 scores to New Mexico and New Mexico Normal (now New Mexico Highlands) and 36-0 to Texas Mines (UTEP). Along with the thrashing of New Mexico, New Mexico State rolled to victory against New Mexico Normal, 56-6, and defeated Texas Mines, 7-0.

The Round Up makes a strong case for runaway overconfidence tripping up Hines and the Aggies. The story begins with the following tip of the sombrero to the Mustangs: "A determined and inspired Silver City Teachers College football team played the New Mexico Aggies to a standstill the first half and then successfully stopped the three scoring threats made by the desperate Hinesmen in the second half, to completely upset the dope bucket in the game played on Quesensberry Field last Friday, which ended in a scoreless tie.

"The Silver City team, playing a brilliant defensive game, stopped the Aggie offense and piled up 128 yards from scrimmage to 113 by the Aggies, and divided evenly with their opponents on first downs with eight first downs each. The Mustangs outplayed the Hines coached men the entire first half and made 85 yards from scrimmage to the Aggies 35 yards, and six first downs to two for the State college team.

"The Mustangs played heads-up football during the entire game, but were unable to make good their best scoring chance which came in the last few minutes of the game as the result of a recovered Aggie fumble on the Aggie 22 yard line. The Aggies immediately regained possession of the ball by intercepting a Mustang pass.

"The center of the teachers' line was the strongest part of the game, and Davis, left end playing his second game of the season, was responsible for many tackles. Walter Nations and Emmett Hixon played the most consistent game for the Aggies in the line, and Lauro and Hookey (sic) Apodaca did the most outstanding ball carrying and pass receiving for the Hinesmen."

Then, in an oh-by-the-way moment fairly deep into the story, a significant point is mentioned.

"Coach Jerry Hines started his second team against the Mustangs and played them for the entire first quarter, but he replaced them when it became apparent that there was a lack of offensive drive and that the Silver City team was gradually creeping up on the Aggie goal line," the reader is told in a casual, off-hand manner. "The first string was only able to hold off the teachers, and showed no more offensive strength than the starting team."

A quieter era

If this happened 80 years later, with rampaging radio talk-show experts and take-a-shot-at-whomever-you-wish social media, the outcry would be deafening. In 1935, in his "This And That About Sports" column in *The Round Up*, Johnny Cunningham was supportive and decidedly soft.

"We have no alibis to make for the game last Friday," he wrote. "The Aggies have a good team, but they could not best the Mustangs.

"Many local fans were very much disappointed. They try to lay the blame first one place and then another. However the sports writers of the daily papers are taking a much different attitude and while they feel that it was unfortunate, they do not feel that anyone was to blame and that it does not mean as much as the drug store quarterbacks try to make us believe.

"It was only a natural let-down after the Lobo game, for which the critics were as much to blame as anyone. It was the spirit of the campus that had much to do with the upset. A football team is not a machine, with certain set skill and ability which will function the same at all times. For the Lobo game there was a perfect psychological buildup with victory, and for the Silver City game there was a perfect buildup for over-confidence."

That was as gentle a barb, if even a barb, as possible.

The enthusiasm carried over to '36 with a school record turnout of 42 players. They won their first three games. It was loss-loss-tie in their next three games. Then it was another three-game winning streak. They finished with a slump, losing their final two games. The offense was similar to '35, scoring 252 points for a 22.9 average. It was the defense that slipped, allowing 118 points for a 10.72 average. The Aggies were 3-2 in the Border Conference. Arizona ruled the roost once again, this time with a 3-0-1 record. Hines broke from a long-standing tradition of limiting the schedule to teams in the Southwest when he arranged a two-game series with the University of California, Santa Barbara, then Santa Barbara State College. "My dad loved to go to California," Walter Hines said in an interview. The Aggies lost, 25-14, at Santa Barbara in 1936, and won, 9-7. in 1937 in Las Cruces.

College football has become a full-time job today. Players remain on scholarship during the summer to get ahead with their class work or catch up, depending on what is required. This enables the team to feed them and put a roof over their heads. It also allows such football program employees as the strength and conditioning coaches, along with nutritionists at the more well-heeled programs, to keep an eye on the athletes.

In truth, the strength and conditioning people do more than keep an eye on them. There are supervised workouts on campus throughout the summer. If you could turn the clock back, you would not find players on campus during the summer. They would have gone home, or elsewhere, to jobs. In the summer of 1937, players reported they pushed a wheelbarrow filled with mortar on a construction site, worked in a machine shop, in the Texas oil fields, in a power plant and for the Mississippi highway department. No doubt players of today would consider this an outrageous imposition.

The Aggies were back on top of their game in 1937, starting with a 14-0 victory over Texas College of Mines, later known as Texas Western and now rebranded the University of Texas-El Paso, or UTEP. While their offense was less formidable this season – 128 points for a 14.2 average – their defense was stout as they allowed 60 points for a 6.6 average. The Aggies were 4-1 in the Border Conference, but the championship was awarded to Texas Tech at 3-0.

The story was similar in 1938 when they scored 166 points, an average of 18.4 points a game, and allowed 75, an average of 8.3 points. There was one pleasant difference. They were Border Conference co-champions with another 4-1 record. The title was shared with UNM, which was 4-2. It was hard to quibble about the shared title with the Lobos because they squeezed past the Aggies in a baseball score, 6-2. UNM's losses were at Texas Mines, 7-6, and in Albuquerque against Texas Tech, 17-7. The folks in El Paso, in their infinite wisdom, selected UNM to play in the Sun Bowl game, where it was throttled by Utah, 26-0, on January 1.

The '38 Aggies lost one non-conference game, 12-6, to an Arkansas State team under the direction of a young coach who 20 years down the road would surface in Las Cruces. That was none other than Warren Woodson. The then-35-year-old Texan would return in 1958 to coach the Aggies. His NMSU teams recaptured and then surpassed the success of the Hines years. Woodson's 1938 Arkansas State team was 7-1.

A year later, Hines would take the Aggies to Arkansas State and emerge the winner, 12-3. So it was that Hines and Woodson, the two biggest winners in New Mexico State football history, were 1-1 against one another. Put that one in your Aggies trivia quiz. One of the things that had to be satisfying to the Aggies faithful during this four-year success stretch between 1935 and 1938 was the fact that they had a 4-0 record against Arizona State and 3-1 records against Texas Mines/UTEP and their "friends" from Albuquerque, aka UNM.

With World War II approaching, things looked fine for the Aggies at the start of 1939. However, the team spiraled downhill quickly.

"A lot of guys stopped going to college," Walter Hines said.

Japan bombed Pearl Harbor on December 7, 1941. President Roosevelt asked for a declaration of war on Japan on December 8. Congress did so that very day. Three days later, Germany and Italy, Japan's allies, declared war on the United States.

Football becomes secondary

"Although they say we were surprised by the war, guys were preparing for the military," Hines said.

In '39, after a 3-0 start, the Aggies hit the skids, losing their remaining six games. They did not score in three of those games and had a total of 22 points in the other three. Their totals from this 3-6 season were 93 points scored, an average of 10.3 points a game, and 141 points allowed, 15.6 a game.

This was the last Aggie football team Hines coached. His overall record of 54-36-10 gives him the second most wins of any of the 34 men who have coached New Mexico State football, trailing only Woodson's 63-36-3 record. Of the eight men who coached five or more seasons, only Woodson, Hines and John Miller, who coached all of 24 games, posted winning records.

Walter Hines writes of his father: "Although he returned to campus briefly as a basketball coach in 1946, World War II effectively brought an early end to Hines' coaching career. As battery commander of the 120th Combat Engineers, a New Mexico National Guard unit assigned to the 45th Infantry Division, Captain Hines and a number of Las Cruces men were among the first called to military duty in September 1940 as the U.S. mobilized in preparation of entering the war. They served in Africa, Sicily, and Italy, where Hines was stricken with a heart condition. He returned to the states in 1945 for limited duty as athletics officer at Ft. Bliss."

The 120th was part of the 45th division.

"It was made up of men from Oklahoma, Texas and New Mexico," Hines said in the interview. "Dad was XO (executive officer, typically second in command in an Army unit). They were building training facilities. They piddled around the U.S. before they left for North Africa. I don't think they saw any fighting there. They did in Sicily and in landings in Italy.

"My dad had a heart attack in Italy and came home. The remainder of the group served in the part of the front under (Gen. George S.) Patton's jurisdiction. They liberated Dachau."

Jerry Hines returned to New Mexico State following the war, coached that one season of basketball, and served as athletic director until retiring. Walt Hines, who was about five years old at the time, was not privy to specifics of the separation late in 1948 or early in 1949 (the last time Jerry Hines is cited as athletic director is in a December 15, 1948 story in *The Round Up*). It could have been because of health or a philosophical difference. What he does remember is his father "was bummed," suggesting the elder Hines was pushed out. Walt Hines indicates the key administration figure in this drama was John Branson, who over the years was dean of college, acting president three times and president of the university. Whatever the reason, and however Jerry Hines felt about administrators not having his back, it did not prevent him from sending his son to New Mexico State to earn bachelor's and master's degrees in engineering.

Walter Hines proudly points out his father had a 102-36 basketball record between 1935 and 1940. His teams made it to the National AAU Tournament in Denver in 1936, the National College Basketball Tournament in Kansas City in 1938 (sanctioned by the NAIB, which became the NAIA in 1952) and the NIT Tournament in Madison Square Garden in 1939, each of which was a big deal in that era. The NIT team lost to eventual champion Long Island, 52-45. Hines' record running up to WW II was 149-92. He tacked on one additional season, 1946-47, when the Aggies were 8-17, to finish with a 157-109 career record. His 1936-37, 1937-38 and 1938-39 teams, each the Border Conference champion, were 22-5, 22-3 and 20-4. New Mexico State coaches would not get to 20 or more wins again until 1951-52 and 1959-60. George McCarty did it first, with a 22-11 record. That team reached the NCAA Sweet 16. Presley Askew was next up at 20-7 with a one-and-done NCAA Tournament team. There would not be repeat 20-plus-wins seasons until another former New Mexico State player, Lou Henson, coached the team, then an independent without a conference affiliation, to 23-6, 24-5 and 27-3 seasons starting in 1967-68. Those teams went to the Sweet 16 the first two years and the Final Four in 1969-70, losing to eventual champion UCLA, 93-77.

The UNM rivalry, aka the Rio Grande Rivalry or the Battle of I-25, brings NMSU football as well as the Hines years into focus. Merriam-Webster defines rivalry as "a state or situation in which people or groups are competing with each other." When Hines played, from 1922 to 1925, his teams went 3-1 against the Lobos. The rivalry was 10-10-2 when Hines took over as coach. He nudged the Aggies ahead, having gone 5-4-2, to leave them with a 15-14-2 series edge when he went off to war.

Walker 3-1 against Lobos

Hines lost his last two football games against UNM, an indication of what was in store for the Aggies. Eight coaches — Julius Johnson, Maurice Moulder, Babe Curfman, Vaughn Corley, Joseph Coleman, James Patton, Tony Cavallo and Woodson — extended the losing streak to 18 games before Woodson, in his second

An undated photo of the Aggie football team (Courtesy of New Mexico State University Archives and Special Collections Department)

season at the helm, took control with a win against the Lobos. Woodson would go 6-4 against UNM. There have been 10 NMSU coaches since President Roger Corbett parted company with Woodson. All have had losing NMSU career records. Only DeWayne Walker, who had an otherwise unimposing 10-20 four years running the program, had a beat-UNM formula. Walker's teams prompted some smiles in the desert, winning three with one loss against the Lobos. The one-time rivalry now stands UNM 67, NMSU 31 with five ties. So much for competing. UNM has dominated the series by a 53-16-1 count since the departure of Hines.

The brothers Mechem, Jay and younger sibling Ed, were among Jerry Hines' Aggies. "Jay was a very good player," Walter Hines said. "He played basketball and football; he was 6-2 and over 200. He was killed on Luzon in the Philippines. He was a colonel." Ed Mechem went on to become a three-time governor of New Mexico, chief executive of the state numbers 15, 17 and 19. He also was a member of the New Mexico House of Representatives, a U.S. Senator and a federal judge. He earned his law degree at the University of Arkansas. What he was not was quick. "Dad said he was kind of slow," Hines said. "He loved to play football." The bond between coach and player was clear down the road. "When Ed was governor, he was the best man when Dad remarried after my mother died," Walter said.

Another memorable player was Jack Lee. "He was one of the last guys in the '30s to play without a helmet," Hines said.

The Walter Hines history tells us, "By 1933-34, the Aggie athletic program was on the upswing. Vaughn Corley, fresh from his success at Las Cruces High, was hired as an assistant to Coach Hines. Corley, who was in the first graduating class at Texas Tech, was pivotal in developing freshman teams in both basketball and football. He was also a trackman, and introduced track and field as a real varsity sport with obvious benefit to both the football and basketball programs. Cigar-chomping wheeler-dealer Dan Williams, a crony of the new Democratic Governor Clyde Tingley, made the scene as a regent in 1933. Williams was also the County Road Superintendent, a powerful patronage-granting position in its day. He soon became President of the Board of Regents and led the much-needed drive for better facilities and funding for Aggie athletics."

NMSU football no longer was the quaint activity it had been in the early years when the opposition was likely to be El Paso High School, Fort Bliss or Albuquerque (probably a town team). Or the El Paso Athletics. Or the Albuquerque Athletics. At late as 1925 and 1926, the Aggies continued to play high school teams. They opened the season in '25 with a resounding 44-0 win over Las Cruces High, and a tighter 7-0 win over El Paso High. They continued to mix in junior colleges on their schedule into 1936 when they actually lost to New Mexico Military, 13-6.

Jerry Hines was saluted by New Mexico State University when he was inducted into the inaugural Aggie Athletic Hall of Fame class in 1970.

CHAPTER FIVE
In the Beginning — Sun Bowl 1936

The Rose Bowl salutes itself as "The Granddaddy of Them All" because it was the first bowl game played, in 1902. It was a 49-0 Michigan win over Stanford, leaving the organizers in Pasadena so humiliated they passed on football for chariot races, ostrich races and sundry other events. They returned to football in 1916 and have held their game annually since.

The Sun, Sugar and Orange Bowls joined the party in 1935. The Orange Bowl led off with Bucknell defeating Florida, 26-0, while it was Tulane over Temple, 20-14, in the Sugar Bowl. The Sun Bowl was less ambitious, going the high school route (some will say Texas high school football was a bigger deal than many college programs in the state) with the stars of El Paso High, Bowie High, Austin High and Cathedral High playing together as the El Paso All-Stars. They defeated Ranger High of the town of Ranger, located midway between Abilene and Fort Worth, 25-21. This game, witnessed by a crowd of 3,000, and the following two Sun Bowl games were played at El Paso High's Jones Field.

The Sun Bowl graduated to the college level in its second year with the call going out to New Mexico A&M, now preferring to call itself New Mexico State College, and Hardin-Simmons.

An editorial in the November 27, 1935 edition of *The Round Up*, signed by K.E., discussed the situation. He (possibly she?) wrote:

"Since the Homecoming game, there has been a great deal of discussion concerning the possibility of the Aggies playing in the Sun Bowl New Year's day. The El Paso *Herald-Post* has been more or less sponsoring this idea, and many El Pasoans feel that the Aggies should be invited.

"Arizona has decisively defeated New Mexico (State), and therefore has a clear title in the (Border) Conference championship. However, the Bowl committee is considering the Aggies seriously since we play a more representative schedule than any other loop team.

"Furthermore, with the Aggies playing, there would be the next thing to a local interest angle since a large number of fans from Southern New Mexico would attend. Arizona will probably not be able to play because it has one post-season game scheduled, and it is uncertain if faculty permission for two post-season games can be obtained.

"The advertising this College would receive would be tremendous. A large block of seats have already been sold and 5,000 additional seats are being built.

"The Sun Bowl promises to grow into quite a spectacle, and it seems that it would be wise to accept an invitation, if extended."

It is impossible not to speculate that the proximity of Las Cruces to El Paso versus distance between Tucson and El Paso, 48 miles to 271 miles, and therefore the probability of more New Mexico State fans than Arizona fans attending the game, influenced Sun Bowl Committee members when they extended the invite to the Aggies.

In 1935, New Mexico State, by whichever name you chose to call it, was definitely the favorite of those who cheered underdogs. Arizona was the big boy on the Border Conference block with a lusty enrollment of 2,471. By contrast, New Mexico State was the smallest member of the conference with an historic high of 533 students, including one fellow who was a graduate student. There were 375 men and 158 women. When the deed was done officially and New Mexico State was invited to the Sun Bowl, the headline in *The Round Up* read: "Hinesmen Will Be Border Conference Representatives."

An interesting window into how things worked on college campuses in the first half of the 20th century is provided by the special assembly in which the New Mexico State student body confirmed the acceptance of the Sun Bowl invitation. The only people college athletic directors consult today beyond their presidents and deep-pocket boosters are television executives.

In what was called a unanimous vote, students supported playing in the game and changing the academic calendar so their Christmas break would start December 14 instead of December 20, as listed in the college catalog, to enable them to return to campus for classes December 30. They then would be off January 1 to go to the game. Although Hardin-Simmons had lost to Baylor, Texas Tech and SMU, *The Round Up* pumped the Cowboys up by saying they were "rated as good as Texas University and Texas A&M. While in El Paso two weeks ago they displayed a fine running and passing attack which is as good or better than that of any in the Border Conference."

Actually, that game, on November 23, was played in Abilene. The Cowboys throttled the El Paso school, Texas College of Mines, in what Frank Junell, the Hardin-Simmons publicity director, called "a thrilling 46-0 victory. A week later, in Las Cruces, the Aggies just slipped past the Miners, 7-0.

Junell reported chances for victory against New Mexico State for Hardin-Simmons, which he alternately called the Cowboys, Cowhands, Wranglers and Ranchers, "picked up when big Ed Cherry, a 190-pound bullback, who has been on the injury list for a month, reported for practice." Calling Cherry a bullback was either Junell's way of indicating he was a hard-running back, or it was a typo. Details of the injury were not disclosed.

Pratt, L. Apodaca, George and more all-conference

The Aggies cheered when five of their number were on the official All-Border Conference selected by the coaches. Quarterback Lemuel "Lem" Pratt, halfback

Lauro Apodaca, and guard Anthony George were first team. End Anasticio "Hooky" Apodaca, Lauro's cousin, and center Hugo Master were second team. Master, first team on the Albuquerque *Journal* All-Conference team, was elected honorary captain for the season in advance of the Sun Bowl.

Walter Hines can provide a mini-scouting report on players via comments from his father.

"He talked mostly about Pratt and (Joe) Yurcic," Walter said. "Pratt was not a big guy. He was acrobatic. He'd be running with the ball, a tackler would approach and he'd do a flip to avoid the guy. He talked about how strong Yurcic was, that he was a force in the line. He was 6-feet and 210 pounds. (That no doubt would have made him one of the bigger players on the field during this era.) There's a picture in The Game sports bar in Las Cruces of Yurcic throwing the shot that gives you an idea of how big he was."

Back to the bowl games. There were seven football games on January 1, 1936. The Rose Bowl, as befits Granddaddy, was the big draw with a crowd of 85,000. The East-West College All-Star Game in San Francisco, then a big deal, drew 60,000, followed by the Sugar Bowl at 35,000. The Sun Bowl claimed almost 12,000 (downgraded in later years to 11,000), as did the Poi Bowl in Honolulu. Holding up the end of the pack came the Detroit Lions-Professional All-Stars with a crowd of under 11,000 in Denver and Catholic University-Mississippi in the Orange Bowl with 10,000.

Remember the 2007 Fiesta Bowl game when Boise State upset Oklahoma, 43-42, via a hook-and-ladder pass-lateral touchdown plus a PAT kick to tie the game with 0:07 remaining, and then won in overtime after the teams matched touchdowns (Oklahoma kicked the PAT) with a statue-of-liberty two-point conversion?

New Mexico State pulled a wild card play of its own out of its sleeve to tie favored and bigger (188-pound average in the line to 175-pound average) Hardin-Simmons, 14-14, in the Sun Bowl.

Hardin-Simmons won the statistical war with 302 total yards to New Mexico State's 204. The Cowboys dominated on the ground, 210 to 83 yards. That generally was an indication who won the game in those days. The Aggies did have the edge in passing, 121 to 92 yards. The equalizer, beyond the wild card play, was turnovers. Hardin-Simmons fumbled seven times, five of which were recovered by New Mexico State. The Aggies fumbled three times, losing only one. The Aggies had four interceptions to one by the Cowboys. That's New Mexico State with nine takeaways to Hardin-Simmons' two. The plus-7 quite obviously leveled the playing field.

There were 29 punts, which was an NCAA record.

The Cowboys scored first, in the second quarter. The Aggies matched them before halftime on a one-yard run by fullback Mark Spanogle. Hardin-Simmons reclaimed the lead after intermission on a one-foot plunge by T. Burns McKinney, who in 1937 would become Hardin-Simmons' first Little All-America selection. The Aggies blocked the point after touchdown. Just one problem. They were offside. The Cowboys converted on their second try and took a 14-7 lead into the fourth quarter. This was a point that would come back to haunt New Mexico State.

It was said Spanogle was bothered by what in those days was called a trick knee. The fact that he was back for the 1936 season and did not letter seems to indicate he more likely had something along the lines of a torn ACL.

The Aggies did a little haunting of their own in the fourth quarter. No, make that a lot of haunting.

This is when the Apodaca cousins, who were coached in basketball as well in football by Jerry Hines, and Pratt pulled out their ace from what Hardin-Simmons no doubt felt was a stacked deck.

Pratt, the quarterback, passed to Hooky Apodaca on the Cowboy 35. Hooky Apodaca immediately threw what is described as a long lateral pass to Lauro Apodaca. Lauro Apodaca then did the honors with a 35-yard sprint to score. Hooky Apodaca kicked the final point of the game to seal the tie.

Pratt was the all-purpose Aggie. Along with passing and running, he returned punts, returned kickoffs and punted. A budding bard in *The Round Up* penned the following prose about him: "Replacing Lem Pratt, platinum-haired ace, will be the biggest task facing Coaches Jerry Hines and Vaughn Corley when the 1937 model Crimson grid machine takes to the practice turf for their initial workout this afternoon.

"Gridmen like Pratt – who, teamed with Lauro Apodaca, formed the greatest brace of backs in the league – come only once in every decade or so, but Hines has several men in uniform that may keep the Aggies in the conference grid scramble."

The Round Up reported 20 members of the team were awarded letters. That's from the 29 men, including nine returning lettermen, who reported for the first day of practice on September 10, 1935. Actually, the players were awarded varsity sweaters at a meeting of the "A" Association, the Aggie Alumni Association, which traces its beginning to 1898. Varsity sweaters. How quaint. Sounds like something from a 1930s movie starring Jimmy Stewart, Mickey Rooney, Katharine Hepburn and Judy Garland.

The lettermen were backs Lauro Apodaca, Pratt, Spanogle, Jack Baird and Henry Crownover; ends Joe Hixon, Hayden Wiley, Hooky Apodaca and Clayborn Wayne; tackles Emmett Hixon, Bill Cann, Harry Skinner and Bill Parr; guards Anthony George, Walter Nations, Burton Cline and Bob Donohue; and centers Master and Bob Detterick.

That's 19 players. Someone is missing. Apparently the undergraduate reporter was not a math major.

Another problem involves spelling. There are 18 mentions of Clayborn Wayne in old issues of *The Round Up*. Spell his first name Clayborne and you find him

11 times. So it is Clayborn here. To further confuse the issue, the NMSU *Football Media Guide* lists Clayborne Wayne as a letterman. Hooky Apodaca also is an issue. He is listed in *The Round Up* 51 times as Hookey and only six times at Hooky. However, the Sun Bowl and Walter Hines list him as Hooky. So it is Hooky here. The *Football Media Guide* does a little dance and goes with Anastacio, his given first name. The NMSU Athletic Hall of Fame has it Anastacio F. 'Hooky' Apodaca.

Aggie Athletic Hall of Fame

Both Apodacas and Pratt, along with Hines, have been enshrined in the Aggie Athletic Hall of Fame. Each was in the first Hall of Fame class.

Pratt played on the 1934-35-36 teams. An All-Border Conference selection each year, he is considered the outstanding New Mexico State football player of the pre-WWII era. He also was on the track and tennis teams. He set records of 25.3 seconds in the 220-yard low hurdles and 163 feet in the javelin in 1935.

Hooky Apodaca was All-Border Conference in 1935 and 1936. That's in football. He was All-Border Conference in basketball in 1935, 1936 and 1937, and led the conference in scoring in 1937.

Lauro Apodaca also was All-Border Conference in football, in 1935 and 1936, and was All-Border Conference in basketball in 1937.

Joe Yurcic provides an interesting story. He was a member of the 1935 freshman team, called the rhinie team. He and Fred Logan, a back, were moved up to the varsity for the Sun Bowl. They did more than provide practice fodder during preparations for the game. They suited up and played against Hardin-Simmons.

Logan punted and had some carries. Yurcic was a major player in the game, according to Johnny Cunningham in his "This And That Sports" column in *The Round Up* edition following the game.

"… we want to mention the work of Joe Yurcic," Cunningham wrote. "The Cowboy coaches picked him as one of the men who worried them the most. Joe, playing freshmen football all season, had never before played against a team of the caliber of Hardin-Simmons, yet he held his own with the rest of them." (It seems fair to assume the sentence included a typographical error and Cunningham wanted that to be "the best of them.")

There would be frequent mentions of Yurcic going forward. He was All-Border Conference in 1936, 1937 and 1938, and is another member of the inaugural class of the NMSU Athletic Hall of Fame. Not all the mentions were serious football situations. In the September 16, 1936 *The Round Up*, columnist Kearney Egerton revealed, "Little Joe Yurcic spent his summer in a stone quarry … he was used in place of a derrick."

Logan is another interesting story. He must hold the record for most years registered as a freshman. Unless he has a couple of twins by the same name. A former star quarterback at Las Cruces High, he first surfaced at New Mexico State during the spring of 1933. Along with football, he used his speed in track, setting an Aggie 440-yard dash record of 53.2 in 1934. At some point, like Pervis Atkins, the All-American star on the undefeated 1960 NMSU team, he joined the Marines, where he is reported to have played some football in 1934. He is not on the roster for the 1936 football team. However, he is identified as a member of the '36 freshman basketball team.

A possible explanation for his extended time as a freshman, along with his sojourn to the Marines, was his involvement in the Civil Works Administration, a short-lived New Deal program during the Great Depression allowing students to work part-time for 30 cents an hour, capping their pay at $15 a month. Logan was identified as a CWA participant. Perhaps work and sports prompted him to carry a minimum class load. By the time the 1937 football season rolled around, Logan is listed with a group of backfield candidates. In an example of how exploits become greater over the years, he now has gone from playing in the Sun Bowl to having "ran wild against Hardin-Simmons two years ago." Logan surfaces one final time in *The Round Up* in VOL. XXXI – No. 28 on April 6, 1938 in a list provided by registrar Miss Era Rentfrow of 28 seniors, 27 juniors, 25 freshmen and 21 sophomores who made grade averages of B or better in the first semester of 1937-38. So much for modern-day privacy laws. Fred Logan of Mesilla Park is included with the sophomores.

Yurcic is on the roster in *The Round Up* prior to the first game of the 1936 season, listed as a sophomore tackle with 0, as in no experience. At 200 pounds, he is the biggest player on the team. George was listed at both 150 and 153 pounds in 1935 when he was an All-Conference guard. Master weighed 191 pounds, Lauro Apodaca 174 and Hooky Apodaca 160. It is obvious why none of the poets of the press box felt an urge to label them the Monsters of the Mesilla Valley.

Imagine the uproar today

Here's something else for the quaint list: Each new letterman received "two lusty swats with the traditional broom" before being presented his letterman sweater. No doubt the politically correct police would have a word or two about such an action today.

The Round Up, on January 15, 1936, when the Sun Bowl memory remained fresh, had an interesting if somewhat whimsical editorial under an "A HAT FOR BING?" headline.

"Since Bing Crosby did not win his ten-gallon hat when he bet on the Aggies against Hardin-Simmons, because the game ended in a tie, some students feel that the College should buy a hat for Bing and send it to him immediately," the editorial read.

"Aside from being a noble gesture on the part of State College, Bing would be more or less obligated to acknowledge the hat on his radio program, and hence, this would be an inexpensive way to capitalize on some more possible publicity for the College.

"It sounds like a good idea, and should be done immediately – before the Sun Bowl game becomes ancient history."

There was no information on such matters as with whom the bet was made, what prompted Gonzaga dropout Harry Lillis (Bing) Crosby to bet on the Aggies or what happened to the proposal to present him with what he in his inimitable style no doubt would have referred to as a rather large Panama, beret or, most likely, a 10-gallon chapeaux.

On a more serious note, on February 5, "K.E." wrote, "The fact that New Mexico State College athletes have outworn the present facilities is an established fact, but the thought of their hurting our relations with other schools and the reduction of gate-receipts has not entered most of our minds. Many fans were not able to see the Arizona-Aggie (basketball) series due to the large crowd that packed into the gym and those not on the front row had the game completely obscured. The reserved seats on the first floor are too close to the court and paying customers have to cope with the problem of keeping players off their necks. The gym is a fire-trap and in case there should be a blaze, the few exits could not handle a mob such as attended the Arizona series.

"The Wildcat coach stated before the game that Arizona would never play another game here unless we get a new gym. The players were handicapped by the small floor and the over-hanging balcony.

"The athletic department realizes the harm being done by these things and for years Coach Hines has been pressing for a new gym. Since the Sun Bowl game, Governor Tingley has shown much interest in us, and no time should be lost by all of us, with the cooperation of the uptown business men, in leaving any stone unturned until the new gym is a reality."

Two additional notes, one on basketball, one on football, both from Cunningham in his column in *The Round Up* on December 11.

"Many think that the basketball team will suffer as a result of the Sun Bowl game," he wrote. "While many of the conference teams started practice before the end of football season and they are all in full swing now, we feel that the basketball men will have time to round into good shape. The men who are not on the football team are already practicing and the ones who are on the football squad will be in good physical condition. Most teams do not get settled down to serious practice until after Christmas, unless games have been scheduled for the holidays.

"An effort will be made at the conference meetings Saturday to postpone the Texas Miners games to January 10 and 11 and to move the Tempe (Arizona State) game to a later date. If the team has a successful season, Jerry (Coach Jerry Hines) plans to take the team to the National A.A.U. tournament at Denver in the spring."

The football-basketball overlap was not a problem for Hines. His 1934 basketball team was 10-9 followed by a 12-6 record in 1935. The 1936 team would be 10-9 again followed by a run of success with 22-22-20 wins. Those teams were back-to-back-to-back Border Conference champions. As for the 1935 schedule, they were forced to play UTEP, then Texas Mines, on January 10 and 11 in El Paso. The Aggies won each of those games, thank you.

Cunningham could not resist some sophomoric cheerleading with his second subject.

"The Aggies can come out on top in the biggest football event in football history at New Mexico State, the Sun Bowl game, if the team is given enough cooperation and support," he wrote. "The game itself is an honor for both the team and the college and if New Mexico State comes out on the long end of the score it will mean more for the College than any other one thing in its history."

On Jan. 8, Cunningham took on his elders in the state print media with the following:

"Although New Mexico daily newspapers chose to almost completely ignore the Sun Bowl game, the Aggies received far more publicity for this game than from anything they have ever done. For the first time they received a write up on the sport page of *The New York Times*. The news story appearing in the Jan. 2 edition of the *Times* was just as long as the story of the University of Southern California-University of Hawaii game."

How about that?

CHAPTER SIX
In the Beginning — 1940 to 1957

The foundation Jerry Hines put in place during the 1930s crumbled to dust in the 1940s and deep into the 1950s.

That's dust as in during 15 seasons from 1940 to 1957 New Mexico State endured 15 losing seasons. Six coaches could not turn the tide. The overall record during the disappointing stretch was a dismal 34-109-1.

An explanation is in order. The 18 years from 1940 to 1957 are reduced to 15 for a reason. The 1943 season is ignored because the team was a group of soldiers training at the school rather than your standard issue undergraduates. The GIs played other teams of soldiers from Army bases. The 1944 and 1945 seasons were canceled as attention, energy and manpower were devoted to World War II.

Hines himself set the tone for what was to come with a 3-6 record in 1939 before marching off to WWII. At least the '39 Aggies were consistent. They started the season 3-0 and closed out 0-6.

Julius Johnston, who spent his student years at Oklahoma State, followed Hines as coach. He came to New Mexico State as the replacement for Vaughn Corley when Corley left to become the line coach at Oregon. Had Corley remained, he would have been in line to become coach after Hines. But the door he closed when he departed did not remain bolted. He returned in 1948 to coach the Aggies. Johnston came from Cameron State Agricultural College, a junior college in Lawton, Oklahoma, where he was football and basketball coach. In seven years there, his basketball teams won conference championships five times. His football teams either won or were runners-up in the conference during each of his last five years.

In Las Cruces, it was three-two-one in the wins department for Johnston. He cobbled together 3-6, 2-7 and 1-8 records with the Aggies for an overall 6-21 record during the 1940-41-42 seasons. His Border Conference performance was worse --- 1-4, 0-6, 0-6 for a 1-16 total.

Although attributed to Johnson in the Football Media Guide, Hines was still there to coach the first two games of 1940, a 12-0 win over Western New Mexico and a 10-0 loss to Howard Payne. This makes Johnston's adjusted record 2-5 in 1940 and 5-20 during his three seasons. During his seven 1940 games, the Aggies scored 83 points while giving up 190.

After the two wins to start the '41 season, Johnston demonstrated his own unfortunate consistency, losing seven in a row. Then a brief positive hiccup with a 27-6 victory over New Mexico Western followed by eight more losses. Not that anyone is counting, but that's one meager win in 16 games. In Border Conference competition, or lack thereof, his last 14 games were losses.

Johnston was the assistant coach to Hines until Sept. 28 of 1940. That's the date when (a) Hines was ordered to report to active duty with the New Mexico National Guard and (b) Johnston took over as head coach. And that's Johnston was the assistant coach because there is no indication Hines had a second assistant. Another indication why the going was so rough during the Johnston years was the too-little, too-late factor. Seven new players checked out uniforms the week of September 11, increasing the roster to the grand total of 28 players. As if Johnston did not have enough on his plate, he also assisted athletic director Bud Laabs managing intramural sports and taught first aid and life saving at the pool. His wife was something of a campus social butterfly. *The Round Up* reported Mrs. Julius Johnston was one of several patronesses honored at a Zeta Tau Alpha sorority tea. She was a chaperone at the annual Greek Ball. She and Coach Johnston entertained members of the varsity basketball team with a Friday night supper at their home in Las Cruces. That was life on (and off) campus in the early '40s.

There was more involving the coaches, their wives and students. On Nov. 19, 1939, Mr. and Mrs. Julius Johnston and Mr. and Mrs. Gerald Hines were chaperones for the W.A.A. (presumably Women's Athletic Association) at the La Posada Hotel at Radium Springs, about 21 miles north of campus.

From *The Round Up*: "Shuffle board, ping-pong, horse shoes, croquette and other games were played by the crowd during the afternoon and were thoroughly enjoyed judging from the laughter and gay spirit of the W.A.A. girls and their escorts. Riding burros around the countryside also proved to be a gay sport.

"Everyone had a hearty appetite by the time the dinner was served, but they were well fortified with barbecued beef, beans, potato chips, coffee, buns and cookies.

"After the barbecue there was dancing and card games at the La Posada."

Johnston also coached the New Mexico State basketball team during the 1940-41 and 1941-42 seasons, once again taking over from Capt. Hines. His records were 14-12 and 8-18.

There was more negative stuff to prompt grumbling. Johnston's first football loss in 1942 was 53-0 against Arizona. His final loss of that season and his New Mexico State career was 61-6 to the guys from El Paso, Texas Mines. That's 114 points against the Aggies and 6 points for the Aggies in two games.

Players depart, coach told to do likewise

Johnston was gone after the 1942 football and 1943 basketball seasons, off to Lawton, Oklahoma, reversing Vaughn Corley's journey, to coach the town's high school football team. There he rediscovered the joy of victory, losing only one game in the 1943 season.

There is an ambivalent report about the 1942 team in Jack Howard's "Sports Kolyum" in the Dec. 9 edition of *The Round Up*.

"The '42 football season has been completed, and little remains on our campus in evidence of our poor showings save some half-healed bruises on the anatomies of the loyal squadsmen and a bitter taste in the mouths of Aggie fans," he wrote.

"Discord in the athletic department is probably the influencing factor in several topnotch players' decisions to transfer elsewhere or go home in midseason. ..."

Howard added, "... Coach Johnston gets a hearty vote from us for his attitude through the year. Where most coaches would have worn out innumerable crying towels, Ju met the worst of ill-fortunes and bad breaks stoically and did his utmost to rearrange the remnants of his squad to complete a tough, uphill schedule."

Maurice Moulder, a former University of Missouri quarterback, was the next coach. He came from Arizona State-Flagstaff, where his 6-16 record during the 1940-41-42 seasons included two wins and a loss against New Mexico State. Among his jobs before landing in Arizona was as assistant football coach at the University of New Mexico. His 4-0 1943 team, in a war-shortened season, was called the Aggie-ASTP team. That's Army Specialized Training Program. The soldiers stationed at New Mexico State were in ASTP unit No. 3858. Their opposition was four teams from nearby Fort Bliss, the U.S. Army base spreading across New Mexico and Texas with headquarters in El Paso. The first three wins, each played at New Mexico State, were against the El Paso All-Stars, 32-6, Fort Bliss, 21-14, and the 51st Hospital, 27-0. The season ended at the 51st Hospital, another 27-0 win. Howard wrote, "Special credit goes to Coach Maurice Moulder for the splendid line he shaped up in the short time he had to work in." It is noteworthy that the roster size expanded from 28 to 42 players.

In January of 1944, the Army decided to stop competing in intercollegiate athletics. Intramural competition on campus was permitted. Off-campus competition was out. This ended NMSU football until 1946.

On March 15, 1946, Orren Beaty, in an article in *The Round Up*, weighed in on the pursuit of football success for the Aggies for the as-yet-unnamed first post-World War II football coach.

"He'll have some moderately good material to work with, if war veterans on the squad can and will get into condition. But, starting from scratch as he is he'll be extremely handicapped in playing teams such as New Mexico U., which managed to keep a team going through the war because they had a navy unit stationed there.

"By starting now to build for the future, a coach, if given the proper support from all concerned – students, faculty members, the administration and downtown Las Cruces boosters – may be able to produce a strong team within a year or two.

"But, if the college is going to be able to compete on even terms with more-favored schools around the Border Conference and the far southwest, some changes must be made."

More-favored no doubt was code for schools with stronger financial support, a dilemma that would continue down through the years for the Aggies.

"Foremost is the matter of a stadium. Quesenberry Field should be Qusenberry Stadium, and the sooner the better ... a stadium can be used to provide the means for taking care of the athletes needed for future football and basketball teams," Beaty continued.

"By this we mean that underneath such a stadium – built to seat around 5,000 persons – rooms could be constructed to furnish quarters for athletes. A mess hall where a 'training' table could be instituted could also be provided for, and would enable the coaching staff to see that the players were fed properly. All this could be done at little additional expense, and would enable the college's limited athletic funds to be used for other purposes.

"If something isn't done to attract athletes to the school and to hold them once they are here, we'd better forget about intercollegiate athletes – it's no fun to be a loser year after year, even if it does build character – or else reconcile ourselves to degenerating to the New Mexico Conference.

"An all-around sports program, both intercollegiate and intramural, is needed to attract all types of students. That should be what we're trying to do."

With the exception of the Warren Woodson Era, still a dozen years and a half dozen coaches away, this would be, and continues to be, the on-going theme at the university.

The job went to Raymond "Babe" Curfman. Like Jerry Hines, he was a former Las Cruces High coach. He played for the long-forgotten Brooklyn Dodgers of the NFL in 1938. Yes, that's the Brooklyn Dodgers of the National Football League. He coached the Barksdale Army Airfield Skyraiders during the war. The base was located near Bossier City, Louisiana. Moulder, identified as "duration Aggie mentor," was one of the other candidates. Unlike Hines, Curfman did not have the staying power to bring any magic to New Mexico State.

Football returns to campus

Starting from scratch after the two-year football hiatus, actually three years when you consider that the undefeated 1943 team was comprised of soldiers, Curfman managed to win four times in '46. He only won three times the following season. As if rebuilding a program was not tough enough, it was necessary to postpone spring practice in 1947 because 60 pairs of football shoes did not arrive as scheduled. You cannot help but wonder how much this weighed on him when he resigned after his 4-5 and 3-6 seasons and bolted to Lubbock, Texas, where he had been an end and quarterback at Texas Tech.

No, Curfman did not join the Texas Tech staff. He opted to go into the sporting goods business. This was a short-lived career change. He was back in coaching in 1949, as assistant at Idaho, then a member of the Pacific Coast Conference, which now is the Pacific-12 Conference. His 7-11 record at New Mexico State was a precursor to 7-19-1 at Idaho for a career total of 14-30-1.

The '46 season kicked off against the New Mexico State Teachers College Mustangs, aka Silver City. Reporter George D. Fiske made a point in his story in *The Round Up* to let readers know "Coach Babe Curfman refused to name his starting lineup so early in the week but it will look as if Babe's first team will consist of ..." Fiske proceeded to rattle off the probable starters, no doubt gleaned from observing who was on the first team in practice. It is somehow comforting to know reporters squabbling with coaches is not a new phenomenon.

Fiske ended his Sept. 18 story with this little bit of news: "Saturday's game is dedicated to the players' wives who have organized themselves into a rooting section all their own. The wives have been frequent visitors at practice and can be expected to yell until they are hoarse for 'my Johnny'."

Life would be different in college athletics for several years. Instead of dealing with callow youth just out of high school, coaches had to adjust to returning war vets who, horror of horrors, smoked and were married.

Directly below Fiske's story was a report on enrollment at New Mexico State. There were 1,139 men and 271 women for a grand total of 1,410 students that semester, 910 of whom were veteran men and 14 were veteran women.

The stars of those early post-WWII teams were linemen. Guard Frank Burke was third team Associated Press "Little All-America" in 1946 and tackle Raymond Van Pelt was second team AP "Little All-America" in 1947. They were war veterans who originally enrolled and played in 1941. Little had nothing to do with their size. Each was listed at 190 pounds, ample size to play in the line in those years. Little was a reference to New Mexico State not playing with the big boys of college football.

When the Hines-Las Cruces High/Curfman-Las Cruces High connection did not work, the New Mexico State administration did not blink. It tried the same formula again, this time with Corley, another former Las Cruces High coach and a former assistant to Hines at New Mexico State. Also like Curfman, he spent his undergraduate years at Texas Tech. Corley was the second in a small army of post-WWII coaches who paraded through a revolving door. It was Curfman for two years, Corley for three years, Joseph Coleman, James Patton, like Johnston an Oklahoma State product, each for two years and, finally, Tony Cavallo for another three years.

In all, five coaches in a dozen years. That's an average of 2.4 seasons per coach, which is a far cry from establishing continuity. Curfman's 4-5 record in 1946 edged Corley's 4-6 record in 1949 as the "best" season during this stretch. The worst season was Patton's 0-9 record in 1954. Their average wins per season came out to 3.5 for Curfman, 3 for Corley, 2.3 for Cavallo, 1.5 for Coleman and 1.0 for Patton.

Corley became an Aggie institution, demonstrating there is life beyond football. First hired in 1933, he was line coach on the football team (Hines' only assistant), wrestling coach, boxing coach (boxing was on the NCAA list of sports from 1924 to 1960), track coach and freshman basketball coach. He also taught classes, including women's physical education, and founded the New Mexico State intramural program in 1934. Hines was athletic director. Naturally, Corley was assistant athletic director.

The lure of the Pacific Northwest and the Pacific Coast Conference drew Corley to the state of Oregon in 1939 as line coach of the University of Oregon. He was in the Navy during WWII, coaching football at St. Mary's Pre-Flight and serving as athletic director for Navy programs at USC and the University of Colorado. He returned to Oregon following the war, moving from there to coach the line at Arizona. He returned to the Aggies as head football coach in '48, remaining in the physical education department as an instructor and head of the intramural department until his retirement in 1972.

The steep hill Corley and the other Aggie coaches had to climb was never demonstrated more clearly than early in 1949. That was when line coach Virgil Marsh announced his departure to become an assistant coach at Phoenix Union High School.

"I hate to lose Marsh, but I could not stand in his way for this chance at a better salary then we can pay," Corley said.

When a high school assistant coach is paid more than any member of a college staff it is clear the college is dealing with financial restraints.

Coleman, yet another Texan, from TCU, had the distinction of doubling his wins from year one to year two. The problem is he only won once in 1951. This left his two-win season the following year unappreciated.

When a "win" Is Not a win

To get a picture of how bad things had become, all you have to do is read Oct. 22, 1952 edition of *The Round Up*. An editorial applauds: "Joe Coleman and his football coaching staff wrought some strong magic and got their team into fever pitch for the 'big one.' " The game story starts, "The rampaging New Mexico Aggies won a 20 to 20 game from the Texas Western Miners." Excuse me, no matter how you slice it, a tie is not a victory. That's how desperate the Aggies had become to celebrate something, anything, even a tie.

Hope is said to spring eternal in the human breast. It does in football coaches and undergraduate reporters. Coleman did not have a senior on his 1952 team. He awarded 28 letters, prompting *The Round Up* to opine, "In Coach Coleman's long range building process, the great amount of experience gained by the young gridders will begin to pay dividends in the near future."

Coleman held 1953 spring practice early in March. Late in May, in his role as athletic director, he announced spring sports, dropped because of lack of funds, would be back in 1954. The golf coach was English-journalism professor and, for a while, publicity director J. Paul Boushelle.

Spring sports would be back, but not Coleman. He was replaced as football coach by line coach Patton and as athletic director by basketball coach Presley Askew. Now *The Round Up* weighed in with the following: "The new coaching staff promises no miracles, but gives assurance that they will turn in as good a team as hard work and long hours plus their combined football know-how can produce." The experienced roster, hard work and long hours plus the combined football know-how produced two wins in 1953 and a winless season in 1954.

Patton's biggest win for the Aggies came before he was head football coach. It came in 1952 against Texas Western in basketball. He was the freshman basketball coach at the time. Varsity coach George McCarty was bedridden with the flu, and All-Border Conference forward Jim Tackett could not play in the home game due to a knee injury. Undaunted, Patton took over and notched an extremely satisfying win.

Patton could have used some of those winning points on the football field. His 1953 team was scoreless four times. There was improvement in 1954 when there were only two games in which Aggies did not score. There were some big-time thrashings, 71-0 against Texas Tech, 39-0 against UTEP, 39-0 against Hardin-Simmons and a third 39-point loss, 46-7, against Arizona, all in '53.

Things got marginally better in 1954 after losing the opener 58-0 against Arizona. The biggest margin of defeat the rest of the season was by 34 points, 41-7, against West Texas State. Patton's Aggies scored 56 points and gave up 316 in 1953. They came back in 1954 with 87 points against 306. The two-year total was 143 points for and 622 points against. The averages are 7.9 points scored and 34.5 against.

Things did look promising for Patton at one point. He won his second game, a 12-7 victory over Colorado College. Chickie Lopez, on a six-yard run, and Jim Hayes, on an eight-yard run, scored for the Aggies. One of the exciting plays of the game was a 48-yard punt return by Jim Bradley. Bradley, a four-year letterman (1951-54) from Las Cruces, was a future Aggie coach (1974-77).

Quite obviously, the tale of Patton's two seasons is a sad one beyond wins against Colorado College and West Texas State in the second and ninth games of '53. There was a six-game losing streak before the West Texas win and then the 0-9 '54 season to close the book on him at 1-15. The losing streak continued for five more games when Cavallo took over in 1955 to make it 14 losses in a row.

New Mexico State President Dr. J.W. Branson did not paint a bright picture when he issued a statement which read, in part: "I personally have the highest respect for Coach Patton as a man of character and fundamental honesty. It is also my belief that with general conditions as they are, no coach in this country could have made a very good showing with the competition that our teams have to face."

That was not exactly a ringing endorsement for the potential of the football program.

Dick Mullins, sports editor of *The Round Up*, remained optimistic while acknowledging reality.

"After talking to Cavallo, you would never know that he is the new head coach of a team which has been the perennial doormat of the Border Conference," he wrote in his "Mullin' It Over" column.

"The players themselves are already acquiring a new out-look on life. They are becoming enthusiastic, and realizing that maybe they are capable of playing a top brand of football against a top flight opponent.

"I, for one, wouldn't miss it for the world. I'm going to stick around and see what develops."

What developed did not turn out to be pretty.

Could the new head coach have been in over his head? He came from Glendale High in Glendale, Arizona, where he had been on the job all of two years, winning one league game the first season and five the second season.

Two years as a high school head coach. A losing record. That's how low the bar was set in Las Cruces. Welcome to Aggie football, Anthony J. Cavallo. Don't trip over the bar on your way in.

Cavallo had been honorable mention All-American as a tailback for Lafayette College in 1937. He knew about program turnarounds. Lafayette was 1-8 in 1936 and then 8-0, outscoring the opposition 130-6, in 1937. He had been an assistant coach at Lafayette, served in the Army for six years during WWII and was an assistant for three years at George Washington University, followed by three more years in the Army during the Korean Conflict. Then came his two years in Arizona.

For the Aggies with Cavallo, it was here-we-go-again. He lost those first five games. Then came a glimmer of hope with a 3-2 finish for a 3-7 season. While not all that much to cheer about, it was the most wins since Corley's 4-6 season in 1949. Glimmer became gloom when his 1956 team lost the first eight games of the season before finishing with a win and yet another loss to regress to 1-9.

In the classic eternally optimistic coach mode, Cavallo was full of hope following spring practice in 1957, *The Round Up* reporting he was "extremely pleased with the showing made by his team. He is seeing his football program developing new growth and maturity, and preparing to burst forth next fall into a fine gridiron group. He feels that he is about ready to give the Aggie fans the type ball club they have been clamoring for."

Chuck Boyland, sports editor of *The Round Up*, a true believer, wrote, "Friday night I observed the finest showing of spring football that I have witnessed at A&M in many moons. Coach Cavallo unveiled a mature, confident, and capable team that gave evidence of fulfilling his predictions of two years ago when he began his rebuilding."

It turned out to be less than a half moon. Much less. What was unveiled in the fall was more of the same. Failing once again to fulfill anything but predictions of gloom and doom, the Aggies were 3-7.

In one particularly dismal stretch from the last game of 1955 deep into the 1957 season, the record was 2-16.

Enough was way too much for Roger B. Corbett, who became New Mexico State president in 1955 shortly before Cavallo began his first season on the job.

Cavallo did not tap dance around what had taken place.

"I was brought into the president's office ... and informed in a short statement that for the good of the college my services were being terminated," he said.

His response to a request to expand on his departure: "No comment."

CHAPTER SEVEN
Warren Woodson's Résumé

The hiring of Warren Woodson was a matchup of Bs as in President Roger B. Corbett hiring Warren B. Woodson.

Prior to reaching out to Woodson, Corbett touched bases with Jerry Hines, the popular and successful former Aggie coach and athletic director who was living in Albuquerque. Walter Hines, Jerry's son, remembers long telephone conversations between his father and Corbett as well as the two men meeting on occasion for drinks when Corbett came to Albuquerque for games or meetings with New Mexico State supporters. Football generally and Woodson specifically were topics of these conversations.

An additional source concerning Woodson available to Corbett would have been Vaughn Corley, another former Aggie football coach. He remained on campus in the athletic department. Corley's son, also Vaughn, was an Arizona quarterback during the 1953-54-55 seasons when Woodson coached the Wildcats.

Warren Woodson, athletic director and head football coach of New Mexico A&M College and New Mexico State University 1958-1967.

While the firing of Tony Cavallo was a page one story in *The Round Up*, the hiring of Woodson was greeted with a student journalist yawn. Granted, the don't-let-the-door-hit-you-on-the-way-out-Tony report was not the top story of the day. But at least "Coach Cavallo Out" was on the front page. The story about Woodson was relegated to page three of the four-page student newspaper. It did not even rate the top of the page, that distinction going to the Aggie basketball team losing on the road at Arizona and Arizona State, and student Art Sears fighting for the New Mexico Golden Gloves crown.

There was mention in the story of Woodson coming on board with a 177-72-16 record at the college level, including eight years as a junior college coach. Other sources indicate his record was 175-74-17. Whatever. There is no reason to quibble over a couple of wins or a couple of losses. The point is the Aggies had hired an experienced college coach who was a proven winner.

Roger B. Corbett, president of New Mexico A&M College and New Mexico State University 1955-1970.

The article did not rub salt into New Mexico State football wounds by pointing out that the Aggies had won only 92 times in the previous 27 seasons. In other words, Woodson's success rate was almost double that of the lack of success of the gentlemen who had run the program he was taking over.

The big issue of the day, February 7, 1958, expressed on the editorial page of *The Round Up*, was a response to the *Las Cruces Sun-News* taking a shot at the decision on campus to remove control of the student newspaper from the journalism department and hand it over to, of all people, the students. The opinion at the *Sun-News* was the student staff would lack "adequate and proper supervision," which, not unexpectedly, prompted a response in *The Round Up* under a headline reading "Is That So?" *The Round Up* editorial pointed out the *Sun-News* editorial came on the heels of the decision to shift printing of *The Round Up* from the Sun-News to the *Las Cruces Citizen*.

A second editorial did turn to the athletic department. But rather than focus on the new football coach, the subject was the Faculty Athletic Council. This editorial found fault with the fact that the board was appointed by the administration rather than by the faculty.

Such was the lack of status of football on campus in the wake of six coaches delivering 16 losing records in 16 consecutive seasons.

Two weeks later, *The Round Up*, in an unsigned column titled "sports," applauded the new coach by observing, "After attending the 'Welcome Woodson' banquet Tuesday night at T or C, we are convinced that A&M has acquired a football coach and athletic director whose talents, by all rights, should hoist the old sign gridiron glory hereabouts. 'Coach' impressed us … Warren Woodson is the man to do the job."

The price of admission for the Aggies Booster Club banquet in Las Cruces, including "a plate," presumably dinner, was a bargain $2.50.

The Round Up reported Woodson, never one to tap-dance, told boosters "What we need … enough scholarships to compete in the Border Conference."

This prompted "applause, foot stomping and glass banging."

More Woodson: "This means that the college must give 20 more scholarships than they already do."

More applause.

More Woodson: "Expect the Booster Club to take a big part of the added expense."

Silence.

Woodson, a tennis player, knew the ball was in his court. Any chance this was a preemptive strike? At a later date he could, if he wished, tell boosters they had been silent at the beginning and he expected them to remain so rather than pester him with their ideas concerning the running of his program.

His history signals just such a possibility.

Make that his relatively recent history. At a booster club meeting in Tucson when he was Arizona's coach, he was far from diplomatic, informing the boosters they should run their businesses and he would run his team, presumably without their help. This attitude coupled with back-to-back 5-4-1 and 4-6 records eroded support following a 7-3 record three years in the rear view mirror, making it easy for the Arizona administration to sever ties with him, which is why he was available for Corbett to hire.

Woodson immediately assumed the role of the senior coach in the Border Conference, having previously been the head man at conference members Hardin-Simmons (1941-42 and 1946-51) and Arizons (1952-56). His run at Hardin-Simmons was rudely interrupted for three years by World War II. Following his time as Arizona's coach, he remained on campus in Tucson as a member of the university's physical eduation faculty.

Clearly, it was a different world back then. Can you imagine anyone suggesting to Mack Brown that he remain at the University of Texas teaching P.E. classes after he was fired as the Longhorns coach?

The speed with which President Corbett moved to hire Woodson following the removal of Cavallo makes it clear Corbett knew all along exactly what he was doing and whom he wanted for the job. Speculation the next coach would be a high school coach, such as Reese Smith, coach of the New Mexico Class AA champion Artesia High team, was way off base.

Although such a move was SOP, standard operating procedure, for the Aggies in the past, the still relatively new president had his own ideas about the direction in which he wanted to take the football program. He realized the time when a Jerry Hines could make that jump from high school coaching to the university level was long past. The failure of those who had tried to follow in the large footprints left by Hines made this painfully clear.

Fort Worth roots

Warren Brooks Woodson was born in 1903 in Fort Worth, Texas, the son of an itinerant Baptist minister who ingrained in his son a fundamental religious belief from which he would never stray. Warren played football, basketball and tennis in high school in Fort Worth. A shoulder injury scratched football from his list of sports at Baylor, where he earned his bachelor's degree in a double major, Bible and history, while starring on the basketball and tennis teams.

Having decided he wanted to coach, Woodson then went to Massachusetts, to Springfield College, where he earned a second bachelor's degree, this one in physical education. Yes, Springfield is the same college, associated with the YMCA, where James Naismith invented basketball.

Armed with his two degrees, three majors and unlimited energy, young Woodson embarked on what would be a long and successful coaching career at relatively small, out-of-the-way colleges, which seemed to suit his personality. First, there would be a year getting his feet wet in the coaching profession at San Marcos Baptist Academy in San Marcos, Texas. He moved on in 1927 to Texarkana Junior College in Texarkana, Texas. Long before multi-tasking became a buzz word, Woodson was doing just that, coaching football, track, basketball and baseball at Texarkana as well as football, track and basketball at Texarkana High School.

Woodson crossed the border into Arkansas in 1935 to become football coach at Arkansas State Teachers College, also known as Conway Teachers College because it was located in the town of Conway. It now is the University of Central Arkansas. At this point, Woodson's workload was cut back somewhat. He only had to coach the college football, basketball and track teams. In football, after a 4-3 record his first season, he was 8-0 in 1936 and went on to post a 40-8-3 record in six seasons. Demonstrating his knack for winning in all sports, his basketball teams were 114-40 and won five conference championships, and his track teams won the conference championship twice.

Onward and upward. Hardin-Simmons came calling. Woodson could not resist the lure of Abilene and Texas. Coincidentally, Hardin-Simmons was on the move from playing as an independent to joining the Border Conference. It was not the Southwest Conference, but it was a step up from Arkansas small college football. In a typical game of college football musical chairs, Woodson was following Frank Kimbrough, who catapulted from a 9-0 season at Hardin-Simmons to Baylor, Woodson's alma mater and no doubt his dream job that would never materialize.

Kimbrough did not flourish at Baylor, going 3-6-1 and 6-4-1 in two years before football was put on the shelf for WWII. His 20-0 win against Woodson's Hardin-Simmons team during his first year was only a brief respite. A year later, Woodson/Hardin-Simmons administered a 16-6 defeat on Kimbrough/Baylor. Kimbrough could not find his footing after the war, going from a disturbing 5-5-1 in 1945 to a deflating 1-8 in 1946, after which Baylor bounced him.

Woodson did very well in Abilene, thank you, producing 7-3-1 and 9-1-1 records before spending 1943-44-45 in the Navy.

There should be an asterisk next to the 1942 loss. It was not in a college game. It was not even in 1942. It was 13-7 against the Second Air Force on January 1, 1943 in the Sun Bowl in El Paso. Add a second asterisk for the fact that Woodson was not there to coach Hardin-Simmons. He had been called to active duty as a lieutenant commander in the Navy.

The big games of the 1942 season were forays into the Southwest Conference in which Hardin-Simmons handled SMU and Baylor. SMU was a 7-6 squeaker. But a win is a win is a win, especially when it is a Border Conference team stepping up to handle one of the so-called Big Boys of the SWC. Baylor fell, 13-6. Classic David and Goliath stuff.

The 1942 tie, a scoreless game, something that did not happen often when a Woodson team was involved, was against Border Conference opponent Texas Tech. Thus it was that Hardin-Simmons and Texas Tech shared the conference championship with identical 3-0-1 records. This was a more significant accomplishment than anyone could have known at the time because after WWII Texas Tech would rule the conference roost.

Woodson's first NCAA rushing champion

Also significant, as well as starting a trend for Woodson, was when he turned a sophomore halfback named Rudy Mobley loose to the tune of 1,281 yards, 142.3 yards a game, not only leading the nation in rushing in 1942, but also setting an NCAA rushing record. On the team rushing list, the Cowboys also were No. 1 with an average of 307.4 yards a game.

There was a 10-year span from 1946, when the Border Conference started crowning football champions again following the hiatus for the war, until 1955, the last year Texas Tech was in the conference before jumping to the Southwest Conference. The Red Raiders would win seven conference championships during that period. Woodson delayed the takeover by a year with his 1946 conference championship team. Hardin-Simmons would not finish atop the Border Conference again until 1958, coincidentally the year Woodson started his reclamation project at New Mexico State.

As good as '42 was, 1946 was even better. It was a 11-0 season, including victory over the University of Denver, 20-0, on January 4, 1947 in the ill-fated original Alamo Bowl in San Antonio. Ill-fated because only 3,730 fans managed to find their way to the game, which prompted the organizers to call it quits after that one game.

Veterans hardened by their years of service during WWII became the cornerstone of Woodson's teams. In '46, Hardin-Simmons was, as they say, a juggernaut. Mobley was back at the top of his game, leading the nation in rushing once again, this time with 1,262 yards. The bowl game was the fourth shutout that season. The Cowboys scored 331 points, an average of 30.09 points a game, and allowed 48, an average of 4.36 a game. Having learned their lessons, SWC teams did not venture onto a field with Hardin-Simmons that season. The one "name" school willing to do so was Kansas State, of the then Big 6 (Oklahoma, Kansas, Missouri, Nebraska, Iowa State and KState). The Wildcats were tamed, 21-7. Woodson was saluted by being named Border Conference Coach of the Year.

Woodson to Baylor not in the cards

There was some Woodson-to-Baylor talk after the season, based on Woodson's success and the fact that he was a Baylor grad. It did not happen. Speculation at the time had it that Baylor was loath to go the Hardin-Simmons-to-Baylor route two coaches in a row.

Woodson now was a very impressive 67-12-56 over nine years as a college coach. When Baylor did not come calling, he soldiered on at Hardin-Simmons, going 8-3 in 1947 with sophomore Wilton Davis leading the nation with 1,173 rushing yards, and then scratching away at 6-2-3, 6-4-1, 5-5 and 6-6 before taking his whistle and chalkboard to Tucson in 1952.

The '47 H-S team, second to Texas Tech in the Border Conference, was invited to the Harbor Bowl in San Diego, where it distinguished itself by annihilating San Diego State, 53-0. Texas Tech went to the Sun Bowl, where it lost to Miami of Ohio, 13-12.

The '48 team, although sinking to fifth in the conference, somehow managed to play in three bowl games. First came the Grape Bowl, a 35-35 tie against College of Pacific, then the Shrine Bowl, a 40-12 victory over Quachita Baptist and, finally, a 49-12 win over Wichita. It was a traveling circus with the games December 4 in Lodi, California, December 18 in Little Rock, Arkansas and December 30 in Lafayette, Louisianna. Hardin-Simmons flew to those games in a converted WWII Army transport plane. No doubt the players would have called it a rickety WWII Army transport. It also no doubt brought back memories of the war years because it was not a new experience for many on board. All they were missing were fatigues and combat boots.

The fact that Woodson's last two Hardin-Simmons teams were 11-11 overall, did not stifle the imagination of the brass at the University of Arizona. They locked in on Woodson's record at Hardin-Simmons against their Mildcats. Excuse me, that's Wildcats. His teams handled Arizona more often than not, winning five of the seven times they met. He was even more successful against rival Arizona State, pounding the Sun Devils by such scores of 20-0, 46-6, 42-0, 63-25, 34-13, 41-14 and 39-14 on his way to an 8-0 record against them (one win was a forfeit).

Football seemingly was on the upswing in Tucson under Coach Bob Winslow. In his three years, his teams improved from 2-7-1 to 4-6 to 6-5. Just one problem. But it was a big one. Winslow was 0-3 against Arizona State. Making matters even worse, the margin of defeat was expanding from 27 points (34-7) to 34 (47-13) to an oh-my-gosh 47 (61-14).

Seeking to become much more wild than mild, Arizona lured Woodson out of Texas. He was leaving a small (around 2,000 undergraduates), private, church-affiliated school founded as Abilene Baptist College by the Southwestern Baptist Association for the growing public state flagship university.

Victory Offense, the complete manual for winning with the T-formation, is a book written by Warren Woodson.

Woodson had become a trendsetter in Texas with his high-powered wing-T offense. Why not in Arizona?

Well, it takes more than talk. And hope. And theories. And more hope.

With the exception of brief interludes in 1952 and 1954, Woodson's approach never found traction at Arizona. His first team was 6-4. While you might be inclined to shrug and point out he did no more than duplicate Winslow's last year, Woodson was named Border Conference Coach of the Year for the second time, indicating he did more than the selection jury expected.

Moving forward, his Arizona teams were 4-5-1, 7-3, 5-4-1 and 4-6 for an uninspiring 26-22-2. His teams fared no better in the Border Conference, going 3-2 for each of his first three years to finish third, fourth and fourth, before slipping to 1-2-1 (fifth) and 1-2 (fourth) for an even more uninspiring 11-10-1 record.

Where Woodson did find traction once again was the manner in which his featured back piled up the yardage. Art Luppino, called the "Cactus Comet" by an inspired press box bard, provided him with his fourth and fifth individual college rushing championships in 1954 and 1955.

USC became known as Tailback U when Mike Garrett, Charles White, O.J. Simpson and Marcus Allen were winning the Heisman Trophy from 1965 to 1981. Penn State was called Linebacker U when it churned out a host of outstanding linebackers such as Jack Ham, Shane Conlan and Lavar Arrington. BYU was known for its quarterbacks. Woodson was Mr. National Rushing Champion producer wherever he took his Xs and Os.

Luppino put Arizona on the college football map, gaining 1,359 yards on 179 carries in 1954 and 1,313 yards on 209 carries in 1955. He was the first player to win back-to-back national rushing titles. (Mobley did it for Woodson and Hardin-Simmons in 1942 and 1946) His yards per carries averages were 7.6 yards in 1954 and 6.3 yards in 1955. He also led the nation in scoring in '54, a national record 166 points, and with 632 kickoff yards.

When they added up Luppino's four year total of 3,381 yards – 382 as a freshman and 327 more when limited by a pre-season knee injury as a senior – he owned the NCAA rushing record.

His most amazing game came in the 1954 opener, his first starting assignment, during a 58-0 shellacking of, oops, the Aggies in Tucson. Did Woodson pour it on for the home folks? Well, he only ordered the ball handed to Luppino six times. That was more than enough. Luppino ran wild, gaining 228 yards for a remarkable 38 yards a carry average. He scored on runs of 37, 48, 74 and 53 yards plus on an 88-yard kick return.

What about Arizona versus Arizona State? While Luppino lugging the ball was nice, the ASU rivalry was and remains the No. 1 priority of Arizona fans. Here Woodson was moderately successful. Arizona State slipped past Arizona in 1953, 20-18. Then it was Woodson's turn, winning by 35-0, 54-14 and 7-0 scores. The roof and a lot more fell in 1956 when ASU won, 20-0.

Woodson fed the fire with his increasingly belligerent personality.

There are those who today think angry, confrontational fans are a product of social media and the ability to tweet thoughts at will, no matter how ill-informed, without fear of having your target look you in the eye and question your intelligence and knowledge of the subject.

Legend has it that Wildcat rooters, especially members of the Tucson Town Cats boosters group, became increasingly agitated and aggressive in letting Woodson know how they thought he could fix all that ailed his team. He responded by suggesting not too politely that they mind their own business, a tactic that works for a coach only when he is winning, preferably winning big. To those paying attention, this was a harbinger of things to come.

Woodson spent the 1957 season teaching those P.E. classes for Arizona while the Wildcats marched in reverse under Ed Doherty, going 1-8-1 and 3-7 before he too was dismissed.

Arizona proved to be a five-year glitch in an otherwise Hall of Fame coaching career for Woodson. He added 63 wins to his career record at New Mexico State during the 1958-67 seasons and a bonus 16 at Trinity in San Antonio in 1972-73.

CHAPTER EIGHT
Setting the Foundation — 1958

It was January 25, 1958. Warren Woodson had been introduced a week earlier as the new football coach for New Mexico State, still officially New Mexico A&M for New Mexico College of Agriculture and Mechanic Arts.

Woodson was back in Tucson, where the University of Arizona had severed ties with him as football coach a year earlier. Now he was severing ties with the university as a physical education instructor.

The Las Cruces daily newspaper was the *Sun-News*. Anyone who paid close attention to the masthead on the front page noticed editor and publisher Orville E. Priestley's newspaper's full name was the *Sun-News* and in much smaller type *Rio Grande Farmer*.

If you forked over a nickel for the *Sun-News* on this particular day and turned to sports you found an Associated Press story out of Tucson quoting Woodson. The wire service reporter wrote "he plans to return to Las Cruces as soon as he gets his affairs straightened out in Tucson."

Woodson would be in Arizona long enough to pack a toothbrush and kiss his wife and young daughter goodbye until they joined him after the school semester was completed. No doubt, he also was there to collect his files of offensive plays.

"The New Mexico A&M job came up suddenly and it was exactly what I wanted," Woodson said in the article.

A cynic would say exactly what he wanted was a job coaching a college football team and that he would have taken a dog sled to Alaska if the university there had a football team and a job opening.

Woodson, having coached at Border Conference members Hardin-Simmons and Arizona, clearly knew the Aggies and their generally hapless football team – they had not had a winning season since 1938, Franklin D. Roosevelt's second term as President.

There was one indication Woodson was not kidding about the move to New Mexico, that he truly expected to be with the Aggies for the long run. The fourth paragraph of the AP story began as follows: "He said he has already picked out a lot in Las Cruces where he will build a home."

How's that for confidence?

Woodson was scheduled to officially start work on Feb. 1. He barely had time to hang some pictures on his office walls before a campus panel called the Big Plan Athletic Committee issued a comprehensive report on the state and future of Aggie intercollegiate athletics. Typical of what happens on a campus, there was not unanimity of thought. Not even close. The 18 members of the committee split into factions. Late in February, they issued a majority report signed by eight members and a minority report signed by six. Four members, including C.R. Bickerstaff and Presley Askew withheld their signatures although they made no secret of their support of the athletic program. Bickerstaff was the athletic trainer. Askew was basketball and baseball coach, plus he was athletic director prior to the hiring of Woodson.

The majority report recommended continuation of the present program while urging renewed efforts to improve the financial underpinning of athletics. The minority report made a thinly veiled call for de-emphasis. This discussion or debate has not abated over the years.

Woodson was hired as athletic director as well as football coach. Officially, athletic director Presley Askew "asked to be relieved of those duties so he could concentrate on the college's basketball and baseball teams." Realistically, those who knew Woodson knew he chafed at Arizona where he did not have the freedom or control he desired. As much as he wanted to coach again, he wanted to coach where he would be comfortable, where involvement of others would be limited to cheering. President Roger Corbett made him an offer he could not turn down.

Published reports seem to indicate the transition from Tony Cavallo to Woodson was, if not smooth and easy, at least business as usual with players scrambling to impress their new coach.

From the *Sun-News* in an unsigned story most likely written by sports editor Abe J. Perilman: "The nucleus of a strong, interesting New Mexico A&M college team for 1958 was shown in Memorial Stadium Saturday night in A&M's spring intersquad game.

"Despite a determined fourth quarter bid by the Red team largely on the passing of Mickey Folz, the Whites took a 27-0 victory.

"New players and old sparkled on the field most of them on the White unit which Coach Warren Woodson had assigned the players the coaching staff believes is the nucleus for the 1958 team.

"The White unit's performance spotlighted what Woodson has said is A&M's major problem to be solved before the first game next September – a lack of depth.

"Top passers in the game were the White's Mickey Alba with three completions of five attempts for 127 yards and Charlie Johnson's two completions of six attempts for 63 yards, and the Reds' Mickey Folz with eight completions of 22 attempts for 89 yards."

A couple of points of order need to be mentioned.

Let's start with Alba. That would be Ricky Alba, as he was identified in the headline above the story, which read, "Ricky Alba Stars." Three completions constitutes a star performance? What was not mentioned until later in the story was Alba threw two touchdown passes, one was 59 yards to E.A. Sims and another to Joe Kelly for 47 yards. That is efficient passing as well as star quality.

Basketball was Johnson's ticket to becoming an Aggie

Charlie Johnson is Charley Johnson. He probably shrugged off the incorrect spelling of his first name, happy as he was to be on the field after arriving that semester from Schreiner Institute, a Texas junior college, via a basketball scholarship. He had not played football in a year. He was told he could take a shot at making Cavallo's football team. Now with Cavallo no longer football coach, he had no idea what the future held for him other than he was getting a good education as a chemical engineering student.

It can be noted that Alba would become a star, only as a defensive back.

The final paragraph of the story explained that "Johnson's quarterbacking and the cohesiveness and spirit of the Whites drew favorable comment among spectators."

Beyond wondering how many spectators were in the stands for the game, and how many beyond a few buddies were polled, this does provide an early hint of Johnson's future. They would learn how to spell his first name.

Johnson scored one of the White touchdowns, on a 7-yard sweep around end. This was an anomaly. He would not go down in Aggie lore for his ability to run the ball. His strength was his passing ability.

Folz, the White quarterback, provides a peek into what was happening as Woodson put his imprint on the football program. This is a read-between-the-lines exercise. Folz, a junior, had lettered for two years under Cavallo while shifting between quarterback and halfback. A little more than a month later, in his *Sun-News* column, Perilman mentioned the returning lettermen – "Bob Kelly, end; Ricky Alba, qb; Joe Kelly, fb; Louis Kelley, fb; Ben Landin, rg; Billy Locklin, lt; George Mulholland, le; Sam Negrea, lg; Jim Worrick, c; and Jim Bickell, re."

Joe and Bob Kelly were brothers, Joe being the older brother. Also, Billy Locklin was and is called Billy Ray by his teammates and friends.

Conspicuous by his absence from Perilman's list was junior letterman Mickey Folz, providing a hint, perhaps only the tip of the iceberg, about a roster housecleaning that was going on with little if any fanfare. There are nods of understanding from those who survived Woodson's purge. It was not smooth or easy or going forward for some players. Some estimate only a half dozen or so players elected to stick around. The actual roll call was not recorded.

It was not just holdovers from Cavallo's team who had it tough. New players came and left with regularity. The 1959 *Swastika* did not tap dance around the subject when it expanded on this Woodson quote: "We've come a long way since September." From the yearbook editors: "Woodson, line coach Tom Moulton and end coach Noah Allen kept only 11 players who went through 1958 spring."

Berley Pruitt was one example. He arrived in the spring of 1958, a strapping 6-3, 215-pound freshman tackle, alternately identified as from Fort Sill, an Army base in Oklahoma, and Greenville, Miss. He was praised as the outstanding lineman that spring. The story in advance of the 1958 opening game, which would turn out to a more-of-the-same 20-0 loss to Trinity, cites him as a noteworthy lineman on the team. This is the last mention of him in *The Round Up*. He is not listed with lettermen for the season or beyond. Just another player who vanished, perhaps in the dead of night. Or perhaps he was given a bus ticket home, as players say happened more than once.

Brittain Hardman's "Calling The Game" column in *The Round Up* highlighted "Carl Hollowell, 6-1, 190, freshman from Andrews, Tex., coming to A&M after two years in the Army. Should be a headliner in college football as he was in service football. Voted most dangerous back in Alaskan Command Conference, he averaged 7.6 yards by making 423 yards in 56 carries. Was All-Army in 1956." Hollowell is listed as a 1958 letterman. And that's it. The leading ball carrier in 1958, Dick Cohee, a halfback, was yet another vanishing Aggie. He gained 566 yards, averaging 4.8 yards a carry, and scored two touchdowns. He was an academic casualty.

On the positive side was a quote about the still virtually unknown Johnson. Woodson called him a "phenomenal passer." Johnson must have chuckled if he read that. Woodson would never share such a favorable scouting report with one of his players. Praise was not part of his approach. No doubt he considered it coddling, a major no-no in his book.

Imagine what coaches at Texas colleges said to their assistants who missed on Johnson coming out of high school in Big Spring, Texas and again at Schreiner Institute, the only football team to have interest in him.

Johnson only ended up at New Mexico State because of basketball. Schreiner dropped football after his freshman season, which seemingly left his career in that sport dead in the water. Without a football option, he remained at Schreiner for his second year to play basketball. Bickerstaff's duties for the Aggies extended far beyond taping ankles and dealing with the normal aches and pains of football players. He was the athletic department factotum, serving as a balance point for the players when the coaches were showing them no love. He also helped the coaches as scout and recruiter.

Big assist to Bickerstaff

Bickerstaff saw Johnson in a junior college basketball tournament, liked what he saw and, presto, Johnson had a scholarship to play basketball for the Aggies, which he did the second half of the 1957-58 season. Although he did not letter, the Aggies, 14-9 for the season, were 10-3 after January. Might Woodson have been paying attention? Might he have seen something that gave him a hint of the leadership quality that would serve the football team so well for the next three years?

This may be too much Hollywood for you. But it does set the scene for an unlikely or at least unexpected sequence of events leading to the success of football that was to come shortly.

With Cavallo out and Woodson in, Johnson had no idea if the invitation to take a shot at football remained on the table. With absolutely nothing to lose, he approached Woodson, who told him when and where to show up for the start of spring football, which he did.

There were several quarterbacks there, each intent on impressing the coach. Woodson had them throw. That was it. No praise or criticism from the tight-lipped coach. Woodson saw something in Johnson that impressed him. When the quarterbacks came back the next day, Johnson was placed at the head of the line, where he remained for three seasons. What triggered Woodson's decision? "I never asked him," Johnson said. Asking Woodson questions simply was not part of the package. It was "yes, sir" and "no, sir," just as it had been for Woodson, members of his staff and for many of the players in the Army.

Johnson demonstrated during his first semester on campus that he was a man for all seasons. With spring football finished, he turned in his helmet and shoulder pads, grabbed his clubs and joined the Aggie golf team. His name pops up in a report about matches, each a loss, against Eastern New Mexico and New Mexico Western. Since golf is a gentleman's game, he was referred to as Charles in first reference in the story. They switched to Charley in second reference. At least they now knew how to spell his name.

Against Eastern, Johnson broke even playing as the second man. An interesting note from that match is one of the Eastern winners, defeating Sam Holguin, was Randy Womack, the national amputee golf champion. Against Western, Johnson was low man for the Aggies, shooting a 77 on the Deming course.

There was an opening on the football coaching staff when Tony Balsamo resigned following the firing of Cavallo. Woodson quickly reached out to Amarillo High line coach Moulton. This gave Woodson an assistant with roots in the fertile Texas high school football scene.

Allen was retained from Cavallo's staff to coach ends and the defensive secondary. Long before the offensive coordinator title came into vogue, Woodson coached the backs and clearly was his own offensive coordinator. Defensive was more of a collaborative effort with Moulton pretty much taking the lead after Woodson set some guidelines.

That was the football staff in 1958, the head coach and a pair of assistants.

Woodson proved to be an immediate magnet for players. Perilman wrote about "a 6'5" left end named Browning Yelvington from Omaha, Neb., who was released from the Marine Corps … and who has been working on the campus in preparation of enrolling in summer school in June. Woodson has known the family for about 30 years and Yelvington's uncle played high school ball for him back in Texarkana high school."

Perilman neglected to mention, perhaps because Woodson neglected to mention to him, the fact that Yelvington played for Woodson at the University of Arizona before becoming a Marine.

Waxing enthusiastic, Perilman wrote, "With Johnson pitching them to Yelvington and Joe Kelly pacing the ground game, no wonder Woodson has a smile or two on his face. Betcha lot of the Aggie opponents are going to be surprised."

Also not mentioned were three direct transfers from Arizona, fullback Sal Gonzalez, center Bill Wallace and guard Ken Hays. Gonzalez was a bounce-back to New Mexico, having been a star at Gadsen High in Anthony, NM. Wallace and Hays were high school buddies in San Antonio. The Wallace-Hays connection there was Wallace's father, Jewell. He was Woodson's first recruit at Texarkana JC.

The Wildcats were apoplectic about the transfers, especially Wallace and Hayes. Jewell Wallace made it clear to the Phoenix *Republic* his son followed Woodson because "I want Bill to play for him." The controversy was cited by Arizona as reason to exclude New Mexico State from its schedule going forward. Not mentioned by the Wildcats was the fact that the two schools had managed to avoid one another since the 1954 season. For his part, Woodson said he was willing to play with one hand tied behind his back. Well, that's not a direct quote. What he really said was if Arizona would play New Mexico State he would do so without playing Wallace and Hays.

Woodson's wing-T offense

When not exchanging cryptic comments with the Wildcats, Woodson was busy putting in the wing-T offense for which he was known throughout the Southwest.

Student journalist Hardman provided fellow students as well as faculty and any boosters interested with this tutorial on the offense: "In the line-up the center, tackles and guards are spaced about two feet apart, the ends three feet from the tackles. The quarterback is under the center. The wingback is a yard outside the end and, of course, back one yard. The fullback is four yards behind the right tackle and the tailback five yards behind the quarterback. This formation, it is believed, puts pressure on the defensive end through running plays and in effect gives the Winged-T team three ends. It encourages a potent passing attack."

The standard offensive setup of the day was the straight-T with the fullback directly behind the quarterback and the halfbacks on either side of him. Woodson's offense was a blend of the straight-T and the old single-wing offense in which the center snap went directly to the tailback stationed from five to seven yards back, much like the spread and shotgun offenses of today.

Woodson was looking to pass 20 times a game, which was considered wide-open football in those days when many coaches fixated on the negative aspects of passing – incomplete passes and interceptions. Woodson was more interested in the quick-strike capabilities of the throwing game.

Teams tended to be right-handed in those days. The biggest best blocker was the right tackle. The best guard would play on the right side. Not surprisingly, bread-and-butter running plays tended to be to the right side. In the current pass-happy era, the most coveted offensive lineman is the left tackle, charged with the critical assignment of protecting the back of the quarterback as he throws 30-40-50-60 times a game. Woodson did not limit his team to what would be identified as a power-right alignment. He could and would flip the wingback and fullback to the left side.

There were multiple sets – ways of lining up – in the Woodson offense. Along with flipping the backfield from right to left, he could and would split one or both of his ends to become what now are called flankers. Or he might keep the end in his regular spot next to the tackle but send the wingback out wide. Or he might flank the end and position the wingback between the tackle and end, making him what now is called a slotback.

Young Hardman, matching the veteran Perilman in the enthusiasm department, wrote, "Though the Aggies are rated as an all-season under-dog, with a new coach, new formation, new material and good spirit the coaching staff as well as this reporter look for a winning season."

He was correct. Just a year early. Call it putting the cart in front of the horse. The 1958 Aggies would win only four games while losing six times. There would be a certain symmetry to the season as they lost their first two games, won a game, lost a game, won back-to-back games, lost another one, won for the fourth time and finished with two more losses.

It was a 4-6 season in which you could use the numbers to draw whatever conclusion suited your fancy. The results for the season: Trinity, 20-0 loss; New Mexico, 16-7 loss; Mexico (National Autonomous University of Mexico in Mexico City), 28-14 win; at North Texas, 43-12 loss; at Western State, 27-24 win; UTEP (then Texas Western), 17-16 win; at Arizona State, 19-23 win; McMurry, 10-7 win; at West Texas State, 39-32 loss; at Hardin-Simmons, 26-20 loss.

The opening-game loss put a hold on high hopes of becoming a surprise team. While losing to rival New Mexico never is fun, at least this loss was only by nine points. Beating Mexico was not a reason to light up a cigar. Truth be told, it was a no-cachet win that might be compared with a bullfight or, better yet, wrestling on television in that the outcome was pretty much ordained.

The whopping 31-point crusher at the hands of North Texas turned all hopes of surprising anyone in 1958 inside out. This disappointment was tempered at least a little by the fact that North Texas won the Missouri Valley Conference championship that season. The Aggies did get their act together, relatively speaking, with two wins in a row.

Unimpressed with a win over Western State and a one-point squeaker over the neighboring Miners? Only if you do not understand two-game winning streaks was the best the Aggies could offer since a three-game winning streak to close the 1943 season. The most recent two-game win streak was in 1957 when the losers were mighty University of Omaha, now the University of Nebraska-Omaha, and equally mighty Western State College of Colorado, located in Gunnison, now Western State Colorado University. Better yet, the win over Texas Western was the first in conference play since 1953 and the first over the guys from El Paso since 1946. One point, 11 points, 111 points, it did not matter, this was a win to cheer about.

OK, the McMurry win was by a mere three points. But, again, it was a win. The thing about the losses to Arizona State, West Texas and Hardin-Simmons was they were by a total of 17 points. Woodson's teams were in the hunt.

Locklin and Joe Kelly were on the Associated Press All-Border Conference team. Johnson, Mulholland and Cohee were honorable mention all-conference.

The yearbook says there were 43 players on the '58 team, 28 freshmen, four sophomores, seven juniors and seniors Joe Kelly, end Jim Bickel and guards Art Hernandez and Sam Negrea. The foundation for the future was being set by 14 young Aggies. Along with Charley Johnson, the players in for the long haul were defensive back Ricky Alba, defensive back Chris Cadenhead, guard Jim Campbell, end Royce Cassell, center Carl Covington, end Bob Kelly, end Ron Logback, guard Allen Sepkowitz, guard Floyd Strickland, defensive back-wingback Doug Veazy, guard J.W. Witt, center Jim Worrick and tackle Don Yannessa.

They were primed for the job ahead.

CHAPTER NINE
Setting the Foundation — 1959

Optimism and Aggie football had been mutually exclusive, words that could not be used in the same sentence without challenging credibility for lo these many years at New Mexico State.

Times were a-changin' in Las Cruces.

A report late in July of 1959 demonstrated the new attitude around as well as in the football program. J.D. Hynes, the athletic business manager, announced season ticket sales for the coming season had not only already exceeded 1958 sales, they had passed the 1,000 mark. For the Aggies, this was kind of like the 4-minute mile, which Roger Bannister had broken only five years earlier.

While the numbers were modest when compared to the big boys in college football – the capacity of the University of Michigan's stadium was 101,011 – they did show that the long-suffering faithful in and around Las Cruces had become believers who were beginning to talk the talk. Better yet, from the financial standpoint of the program, they were willing to walk up to the ticket office and put down hard cash. They believed in what they saw the previous season. They believed whispers about some outstanding recruits. They believed they could see light at the end of what at times had seemed an endless tunnel.

Billy Ray Locklin (second from left) with (from left) J.W. Witt, Bob Gaiters, Lou Zivkovich and Pervis Atkins, his teammates who were looking forward to 1960. (NMSU Yearbook photos)

Woodson had increased the number of football scholarships from 42 when he arrived to 47. Again, modest if you wished to compare the Aggies with the big boys of college football. Still, it was a major step forward for the Aggies.

A standard line from your standard coach is the best offense is a good defense. Warren Woodson was far from your standard issue coach. He wanted to score points and see if you could keep up the pace. It was a reasonable facsimile to fast break basketball, only dribbling the ball was not encouraged. In this area, Woodson was like all coaches. He wanted the pigskin secure.

The starting point of Woodson's recipe with the Aggies was a mature, experienced quarterback who was rapidly moving from raw to polished gem. That, of course, was civil engineering student Charley Johnson.

Woodson also was in the process of adding a full measure of Bob Gaiters and Pervis Atkins, a pair of explosive backs out of the plentiful California junior college ranks, both from Santa Ana JC, located in the growing Los Angeles suburb of Santa Ana in Orange County.

Gaiters was a JC All-American who played his early football in Zanesville, Ohio, before following Horace Greeley's famous "Go West, young man" admonition. Atkins, at this point identified as Gaiter's sidekick, was from Oakland, across the bay from San Francisco, by way of the United States Marines. He was far from a star while attending Oakland Tech High School. Not even close. He was a small guy who would not grow and mature until he served in the Marines. Now he was ready to play. It was clear during spring practice that Woodson had pulled off a recruiting coup and that each new player was the real deal.

Legend has it that Gaiters was recommended by former Aggie Harry Skinner, an Orange County businessman, and that Atkins was sort of a throw-in to entice Gaiters to come to and then remain in Las Cruces. One story has Atkins arriving on campus only because, with nothing better to do, he volunteered to give Gaiters a ride from California to New Mexico. The story continues that he stayed when somehow, quite miraculously, a scholarship appeared for him out of the blue. Atkins himself apparently enjoyed spinning this tale over the years.

Did someone say too much Hollywood?

Would Woodson have had a scholarship for Atkins had Cohee handled his class work and remained an Aggie?

Would Woodson have been interested in Gaiters if he knew he could depend on Cohee as his primary running back in 1959?

A lot of things, unlikely as well as unexpected, were merging. All anyone knows for sure now is the firm of Gaiters and Atkins, soon to become the firm of Atkins and Gaiters, was present and accounted for, and, no matter in which order they were listed, would be far more than adequate as New Mexico State formally shed the A&M part of its name and with it the hang-dog losing ways of the past.

Atkins steps out of Gaiters' shadow

It was Atkins and Gaiters in 1959 because an ankle injury sidelined Gaiters for part of the season, prompting Atkins to slide over from wingback to tailback in Woodson's wing-T formation. Saying Atkins took over in the absence of Gaiters would be an understatement. He led the nation in rushing with 971 yards. He was the fourth Woodson player to lead the nation in rushing and it was the sixth time a Woodson player won the title. For good measure, Atkins led the nation in scoring with 107 points, and in punt returns with 241 yards on 16 carries, an average of 15.1 yards a return. The offense was second in the nation to Syracuse in scoring with 332 points (33.2 average) during the 10-game regular season.

It was pick your poison when you played this New Mexico State team. If you concentrated on stopping the run, the ball was sure to be in the air. Or the other way around.

Johnson led the nation with 18 touchdown passes. He was second in total offense with 1,635 yards. His 1,449 passing yards was fourth nationally. Illustrating the surprise impact when he ran, he averaged 7.5 yards on his 186 yards rushing. Oh, and his 199 passes were sixth, his 105 completions were fifth and his 1,449 passing yards were fourth.

Refusing to be totally denied because the ankle injury forced him to miss four games, Gaiters contributed 490 rushing yards (85 carries, 5.8 average) and 58 points in the scoring column. He was an All-Border Conference selection along with Atkins, Johnson and E.A. Sims, a tower of strength on defense as well as offense at end. Guards J.W. Witt and Jim Campbell were honorable mention All-Border Conference, as was end George Mulholland. It was a repeat performance for Mulholland.

Receiving was spread out with Atkins (22 catches), Bob Kelly (20 in six games), Sims (19) Mulholland (18), Louis Kelley (14) and Sal Gonzalez (8) sharing the load.

Lou Zivkovich had two interceptions, eye-catching for a tackle. Each time, while rushing the quarterback, he deflected a pass and caught the ball before it hit the ground.

No surprise then that Woodson doubled the trouble he was providing the opposition by improving on a four-win inaugural season to an 8-3 record in his second year with the Aggies.

The record in '59 went far beyond doubling '58. The eight victories were more than the seven wins accumulated in the four seasons before the arrival of Woodson. The last impressive season had been Jerry Hines' 7-2 season all the way back in 1938. The only previous eight-win season had been Cap Brown's 8-0 record in 1923 when his quarterback was sophomore Jerry Hines. Among the victims in 1923 were El Paso High (10-0), El Paso Garden Grocers (33-0), Beaumont Hospital

TEXAS WESTERN UPSETS AGGIES

After a week's rest following the 20-18 victory over Trinity U., the Aggies traveled 45 miles south to El Paso for the grudge game with the Texas Western Miners. The Aggies, by virtue of their four wins, 1 loss record were favored over the luckless Miners, but a combination of a good quarterback, (John Runner who went on to win the Border Conference Most Valuable Player award), a determined team, a Homecoming game, and a bad night for the Aggies totaled up to a 20-15 win for TWC. In the first period, the Aggies exploded, as expected, for a 12-0 lead. Taking the ball on the kick-off, the NMSU eleven was forced to punt. Johnson punted deep into Miner territory when their safety fumbled the ball and guard Ben Landin recovered on the Miner 6-yard line. Two plays later Sal Gonzales tore into the end-zone for the score. Villanueva's kick was wide. Near the end of the quarter Bob Gaiters' added another six pointer by going over from 5 yards out. Gaiters then tried to run for the extra points but his effort fell short. In the second period the Miners struck pay-dirt with Furman eating up the last yard. The kick was wide, and the Ag's held a 12-6 half-time advantage. TWC again scored halfway through the third stanza as a fake end run ended in a Williams to De Santis touchdown pass that covered 34 yards. Again the kick was wide and the score was deadlocked at 12 each. Before the fourth period began, Villanueva came off the bend and split the goal-post with a 45-yard field goal to put the Aggies into a 15-12 lead. The Miners wouldn't be stopped though as a last quarter drive put the ball on the Aggie 5-yard line. From there Bradshaw scored and a 2-point play on a Furman to Babbs pass ended the scoring. Gaiters was the big gun for the Aggies as the 205 lb. halfback picked up 124 yards on 19 carries. Johnson completed 16 of 31 passes and 224 yards, but the Maroon and White couldn't contend with the Miners that night.

Gaiters speeds by one Miner while Kelley (44), and Locklin (78) move over to help in game which saw TWC come from behind to win 20-15.

score by quarters:
AGGIES 12 0 3 0
MINERS 0 6 6 8
final: TWC—20   NMSU—15

NMSU DROPS THRILLER TO ASU

In their second Border Conference outing, the NMSU Aggies dazzled Arizona State U. with everything they had in the books, but lack of time kept the Aggies from beating the Sun Devils this year. Between Gaiters, Atkins, and Johnson, it was almost impossible for the Sun Devils to keep ahead in the scoring. In the opening quarter, Johnson quickly put the Ag's in the lead by throwing a 15-yard pass to Gaiters for the first 6 points of the high-scoring game. Gaiters went off tackle for the conversion and an 8-0 Aggie lead. ASU stormed back to tie NMSU the next time it got its hands on the ball. Noland Jones went 1 yard for the score, and then added 2 more on an end sweep. Another touchdown and the extra point put the Sun Devils in front to stay. Early in the second quarter, sub-quarterback Urban hit Rembert with still another touchdown toss, and Jones kicked the extra point for a 22-8 ASU lead. But before the half ended, the Aggies fought down to the one-yard line where Gaiters edged over for the score. Atkins added 2 points on a run, and the Ag's no wtrailed 22-16. Starting the third quarter, Jones kicked an 18-yard field goal for 3 more points. The Aggies countered with Gaiters scoring his third touchdown, and Villanueva booting the extra point. ASU's Jones then kicked another 18-yard field goal, and the Sun Devils now led 28-23. An 11-yard run by McFalls ended Arizona State's scoring after Jones had added the conversion. By now it was late into the fourth period. With time running out a desperation pass by Johnson to Atkins netted 40 yards and the final score of the night. The Aggies worked an on-side kick to perfection, and were on the Sun Devil's 15-yard line when the game ended. The final score read ASU 35, and the Aggies 31. Johnson upped his passing yardage by 264 yards with 19 completions in 34 attempts. Atkins only carried the ball twice, but on a pass receiver he took in 9 passes for 136 yards. Guard Jimmy Campbell was a standout in the line, and of course Gaiters' 20 points was hard to beat. This was the third loss for the Aggies and their record now read 4 wins, 3 losses. However, their Border Conference record was 0 wins and 2 losses. The last time an Aggie eleven had beaten an Arizona State team was in 1938. That year the Maroon and White dumped the Sun Devils 14-12. Over-all performance against the ASU team shows that in 23 games the Ag's have won only 5. But the '59 35-31 loss can't weigh too heavy against the fact that the Aggies finished the game on the ASU 15-yard line.

Bob Langford
Right Half

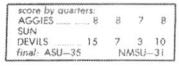
score by quarters:
AGGIES 8 8 7 8
SUN
DEVILS 15 7 3 10
final: ASU—35   NMSU—31

Clem Mancini
Center

(32-6) and Montezuma Baptist College of Las Vegas, New Mexico, identified as Montezuma College (73-3). That's a cumulative score against the Grocers, the Hospital and Montezuma of 138-9. Hardly the competition the Aggies lined up against 36 years later.

The 1959 season began with a 35-0 win over Arizona State-Flagstaff. It was the first win in a season opener for the Aggies since 1952, a year before Dwight D. Eisenhower became President.

Feeling good about themselves, the Aggies went to Albuquerque and in a restart-the-rivalry game defeated UNM, 29-12. This was the first time since 1937 the Lobos had not prevailed. To develop a frame of reference, Charley Johnson and Bob Gaiters would not be born until 1938. Pervis Atkins, the Marine veteran, was a child approaching his second birthday the last time the Aggies flexed their muscles and defeated the Lobos.

A trap in Tulsa

The easy cruising came to halt in the third game of the season, a 28-27 loss at Tulsa. The difference between defeat and a tie was senior third-string quarterback Danny Villanueva's missed point after touchdown (PAT) kick. Villanueva, referred to by the undergraduate journalists as the "Golden Toe," was the first-string Aggie punter as well as kicker. He would spend eight seasons handling both chores in the National Football League, five with the Rams, then playing in Los Angeles, and three with the Dallas Cowboys. His best punting average in the NFL was 45.4 yards in 1963 with the Rams. His pro PAT numbers were 111 of 113 PATs with the Rams and 125 of 128 with the Cowboys for a grand total of 236 of 241, meaning he made 97.9 percent of his PAT kicks in the NFL. As accurate as he was, one went wide in Tulsa. That's how the cookie crumbles, as they say, and how teams lose or, in this case, fail to at least tie a game.

Villanueva — formally Daniel D., or Dan D. Villanueva when he was editor of *The Round Up* in 1959-60 — turned to broadcasting as his NFL career wound down, first as a sportscaster at KMEX in Los Angeles and then in management there, working his way up the corporate ladder from news director to president of Univision. His success in the business world continued in private equities and what he described as family investments with sons Danny Lee and Jim following the sale of Univision. This success enabled him to become a major donor to NMSU. Following his death at the age of 77 in June, 2015, President Barack Obama sent a letter of condolence to his family, *The New York Times* recognized him with an obituary and Tom Brokaw, his broadcast colleague at KNBC in Los Angeles, wrote a letter to the *Los Angeles Times* with some of his memories of Danny.

All things considered, the 2-1 start was not something to complain about. Not if you knew Aggie football history. If you did, you knew there had been five 0-3 starts and eight 1-2 starts since the 3-0 opening run in 1943, and we throw 1943 out because that was service men representing the Aggies. There had not been a legitimate 2-1 start since 1941, and that was the season in which the bottom fell out when a 2-0 start was followed by loss after seven consecutive losses.

This was a positive time with a 43-11 win over McMurry and a 20-18 win over Trinity in the fourth and fifth games to improve the record to an impressive 4-1.

At least things were positive until a pair of chilling defeats in which New Mexico State appeared to be not quite ready for Border Conference quality prime time in a 20-15 loss to Texas El Paso and a 35-31 loss at Arizona State. Suddenly, the impressive 4-1 record had become a much less impressive 4-3.

Returning to the positive, the Aggies closed the season by rattling off four wins in as many games, 42-13 over Hardin-Simmons, 35-13 over West Texas State, 55-0 over unfortunately hapless Mexico and then, most impressive of all, 28-8 over North Texas State in the first return to the post-season Sun Bowl game since 1936. Along with the welcome invitation to the Sun Bowl, the most important development was the bold move of 5-foot-8, 155-pound Bob Langford from halfback to linebacker, and subsequently his first start, against Hardin-Simmons. Undersized though he was, Langford would become the heart and soul of the Aggie defense.

Prior to the Sun Bowl, Woodson announced letters were being awarded to 26 players. The list included seniors Bob Cerny, Sal Gonzalez (frequently spelled incorrectly as Gonzales), Louis Kelley, Ben Landin, Billy Ray Locklin, George Mulholland and Danny Villanueva, juniors Ricky Alba, Pervis Atkins, Bob Gaiters, Ken Hays, Charley Johnson, Bob Kelly, Clem Mancini, Dick Rudzik, A.E. Sims, Bill Wallace and Lou Zivkovich, and sophomores Jim Campbell, Royce Cassell, Carl Covington, Bob Langford, Charles Pettes, Allan Sepkowitz, Doug Veazey and J.W. Witt. Rudzik did not to return for the 1960 season. His unexpected departure was offset by Gonzalez receiving an additional year of eligibility.

Woodson also listed a number of non-lettermen on the Sun Bowl squad, players he said still had a chance to earn letters. If you check the *NMSU Football Media Guide* today, you find Chris Cadenhead, Ron Logback, Floyd Strickland, Don Yannessa and Brownie Yelvington listed as lettermen, stretching the foundation in 1960 to a solid 24 lettermen.

Woodson made an important announcement the Monday before the Sun Bowl. He would add an assistant coach to his staff in 1960. Growing your staff by one does not sound like much until you realize he only had two assistants. The addition of one assistant would make the staff one half again larger.

Yes, things were looking good for 1960. But first there was a bowl game on the horizon.

Co-captains Mulholland and Warrick with Coach Woodson in 1959 look toward the 1960 season. (NMSU Yearbook photo)

CHAPTER TEN

Setting the Foundation — Sun Bowl 1959

North Texas State teams still were the Eagles in 1959. It would not be until 1966, seven years down the road, when they switched nicknames, becoming the ominous-sounding Mean Green. Still, they appeared quite formidable in '59, which is why the Las Cruces *Sun-News* declared they were two-touchdown favorites over the Aggies in the Sun Bowl.

Along with a 9-1 record and a ranking of No. 16 in the nation until unceremoniously upset by Tulsa, 17-6, North Texas State had that 43-12 victory over New Mexico State in 1958. Want more? The Eagles had not allowed a touchdown on a pass during the season and had a potent running game built around Abner Haynes (seventh nationally in rushing with 730 yards and a 6.3 yards average, and fifth nationally in scoring with 90 points).

A number of factors, ranging from the unflappable Johnson to Woodson's experience in bowl games to the return of Gaiters and Bob Kelly from injuries, were ignored in the pre-Sun Bowl forecast.

A healthy Gaiters shifted Atkins back to wingback, presenting Woodson with options he did not have when Gaiters was sidelined and Atkins was at tailback. Kelly's return provided a three-man end corps with E.A. Sims and captain George Mulholland.

Also, with all the attention paid to the offense, the fact that the Aggie defense was tenacious and opportunistic was lost in the shuffle.

The barebones summary of the game has the Aggies winning the first half, 21-0, on their way to a convincing 28-8 conquest.

Gaiters was in top form, gaining 123 yards on 20 carries, an average of 6.2 yards a carry. Atkins was called a decoy as he carried only three times for 15 yards, an average of 5 yards per carry.

The previously impregnable North Texas State aerial defense was no match for Johnson. He threw two touchdown passes as he completed 7 of 15 for 124 yards, and was handed the Most Valuable Player trophy after the game.

From their side of the field, the Eagles had to be grumbling about seven fumbles, six of which they did not recover. The young men from Texas also threw two interceptions.

From the New Mexico State side, it was that tenacious and opportunistic defense. That's how it looked to *The Round Up*, which provided the following account: "Most of the fumbles lost by North Texas State were caused by vicious tackling."

Opportunistic Aggies

The game quite clearly turned on the eight North Texas State turnovers. No doubt, North Texas State considered them eight grumble, groan, etc. turnovers. Just as no doubt, NMSU considered them eight magnificent, glorious takeaways. It's all in the eye of the beholder.

You do not need a lot of imagination to hear the North Texas State coaches screaming, "Hold the ball, Find the handle." And more. Fumbling seven times is a nightmare for any coach. Recovering only one of seven might drive you to lawn bowling.

There was more bad news if you were an Eagle fan. Four of the fumbles came when they were inside the Aggie 25-yard line. The 25 is five yards short of what now is called the red zone, in which a team is expected to score a high percentage of the time. Two of the fumbles and one interception were followed by three of the four New Mexico State touchdowns.

Haynes was unable to keep pace with the Aggies. Perhaps that should be the Aggies pretty much held Haynes in check without shutting him down. He gained a nice but hardly exciting 73 yards.

Did someone say something about being a decoy?

Atkins opened the scoring for New Mexico State in the first quarter on a play that started on the Aggie 43-yard line. Johnson completed a 20-yard pass on the right sideline to Atkins on the Eagle 37. Not satisfied gaining a sizeable chunk of yardage and a first down, Atkins reversed field to the left sideline and turned up field, adding an additional 33 yards to make it a 57-yard touchdown play.

So much for being a decoy.

No doubt North Texas State, knowing what sort of season Atkins had enjoyed, was focused on him, making the dangerous as well as rested Gaiters even more dangerous. As a bonus, Atkins caused a fumble "with a jarring tackle," according to The Round Up.

Later in the first quarter, Kelly intercepted a pass on the Eagle 34 and ran to the 5, where he fumbled. It was one of those days for New Mexico State. Not only were the Aggies playing good football, they were getting more than their share of the breaks, as they did on this play when the ball bounced into the end zone.

There are two versions of what happened next. *The Round Up* has tackle Billy Ray Locklin recovering the ball for a touchdown. According to the North Texas State media guide, it was Dick Rudzik, another lineman, who did the honors by falling on the ball for the touchdown.

There is no dispute over the fact that the Aggies were in command and the Eagles were in big trouble. Locklin chuckles when told about the conflicting reports. He jokes that he thinks he remembers recovering the ball for the touchdown, adding that, at 78 approaching 79, he's not going to vouch for his memory. His tone indicates he knows he recovered the ball in the end zone.

The 1959 Aggie team, the Sun Bowl Champs, gather for a group photo on the New Mexico State University campus. Pictured from front left, front are: George Mulholland, Warren Woodson, Noah Allen, Tom Moulton, Lou Zivkovich, Jerry Melder, Floyd Strickland, Marlen Ream, John Pusateri, Clem Mancini, Carl Covington, Joe Williams, C.R. Bickerstaff, Charles Thompson, Dale Alexander, Chris Cadenhead, Doug Veazey, Royce Cassell, Ken Hays, Bill Wallace, Jim Campbell, Preston Bridges, Allan Sepkowitz, Bob Herron, Ron Logback, Dave Hartzell, Bill Kail, Gary Tubb, Wayne Wood, Ben Landin, Browing Yelvington, Pervis Atkins, Danny Villanueva, Don Yannessa, Dick Rudzik, Sal Gonzalez, Tony O'Hara, Larry Menadace, Don Roberts, Frank Kolezar, John Shamburg, Charley Johnson, Dave Thompson, Bob Langford, Bob Cerny, Bob Kelly, Gary McCarrell, Bob Gaiters, Louis Kelley, Ricky Alba, Charles Pettes, J.W. Witt.

Langford too small? Says who?

In the second quarter, Bob Langford, who would have been undersized in the intramural league at 155 pounds, leveled Haynes, causing a fumble.

This led to an NMSU drive of 13 plays and 97 yards, 51 of which were supplied by Gaiters, 30 of which came on a blast up the middle. Johnson passed 15 yards to Kelly for the touchdown.

Billy Joe Caristle provided North Texas State with some hope in the third quarter with a 49-yard punt return touchdown run. Gaiters regained the momentum for the Aggies by breaking loose on a 44-yard touchdown run.

How pumped up was New Mexico State by the Sun Bowl victory?

In his "Lookin ... with Luke" column, Ed Lucas, sports editor of *The Round Up*, revealed the financial gain from the game was "reportedly around $18,000." That was a major infusion of green for the perennially cash-strapped Aggies.

How pumped up was Lucas by the victory?

He called for building a proper stadium to draw opponents such as (this is his published list) UCLA, Oregon, San Francisco and Utah. He groused about the 1960 home schedule of Mexico, Trinity, West Texas and Texas Western.

"If we are to remain a major college then it would seem we need a major stadium," he wrote. This was low key compared to a Student Press Service report quoting unnamed parties, presumably players in the locker room after the game when "comments were heard that went something like this: 'Next year the Gator Bowl,' or 'Why not the Rose Bowl?' "

Tenacious, opportunistic, successful, excited and very, very optimistic was now the order of the day in Las Cruces.

CHAPTER ELEVEN
1960 — The Perfect Season

"If you handle losses the right way, then losses can be very beneficial."

That's what Mike Krzyzewski, the so very successful Duke basketball coach, said after his 2014-15 team rebounded twice, from a 3-3 midseason slump and then from a loss in the ACC tournament semifinal round. The rebound was as good as it gets in college basketball. The Blue Devils won the NCAA championship, their fifth national championship under Krzyzewski's astute direction.

Astute direction?

Losses becoming beneficial?

Warren Woodson and astute direction belong in the same sentence. No fear of contradiction here.

Krzyzewski was a 13-year-old growing up in Chicago in 1960, certainly aware of Notre Dame, Illinois and Northwestern football but presumably totally unaware of what was going on in the desert with New Mexico State University when Woodson and the Aggies conducted a clinic demonstrating that they indeed handled their six losses in 1958 the right way.

Every coach who has ever droned on about how there are lessons to be learned in defeat can smile and nod his or her head about the turnaround in Las Cruces.

A perfect season does not mean everything was absolutely perfect for the Aggies in 1960. The deal is they were close enough to go undefeated.

Quarterback Charley Johnson provided senior leadership along with a strong, accurate arm.

Wingback-tailback Pervis Atkins was a 9.6 sprinter. Tailback Bob Gaiters was a 9.9 sprinter. Atkins was about speed, moves and big plays at the most critical of moments. Gaiters was a pro-type-steamrolling-downhill runner. They provided explosive TNT rarely seen from a running tandem in the college game.

Ends Bob Kelly and E.A. Sims were another tandem, big and bad on defense as well as on offense.

Linebacker Bob Langford was the mighty mite, the undersized man in the middle who, amazingly at 155 pounds, did a lot more than pester otherwise bone-crushing running backs.

The list of contributors goes on and on from A to Z, from Alba to Zivkovich. Ricky Alba in the defensive backfield. Sal Gonzalez and Bob Jackson splitting fullback-linebacker duties. Lou Zivkovich, co-captain with Johnson, and the rest of the offensive line. And more.

The team was few in numbers when compared to football factories such as Notre Dame, Minnesota, Alabama, Oklahoma and Texas. These schools tended to

Aggie football players relax in Milton Student Center after dinner. (NMSU Yearbook photo)

have 100 or more players in uniform. They could stockpile players because they had the facilities and money, especially the money, to do so. That was not the case at New Mexico State University, where some students lived in discarded Army barracks and the football team had recently been living in a condemned dorm.

Another thing about the big boys of college football in 1960. Their teams were strikingly similar in makeup. There were few if any black players on their teams. Certainly not in the South, not in the Southeast Conference (SEC) or Southwest Conference (SWC). Doors were not yet open at Texas or Texas A&M for the black high school stars from the Lone Star State, which is why All-American defensive end Bubba Smith, out of Charlton-Pollard High in Beaumont, played at Michigan State.

New Mexico State was a football melting pot in a number of ways, in race, in where you came from and in what you studied. The Aggies were black, brown and white. They were engineering majors and physical education majors. They were from big cities and small towns. They came from California, New Mexico, Texas, Pennsylvania and elsewhere around the country. They would become teachers, coaches, businessmen, professional athletes and more.

Woodson struck gold with African Americans Atkins (California), Gaiters (Ohio by way of California), Sims (Texas), Kelly (New Mexico) and Jackson (California).

"The black guys could not play in the SEC," said Armando Alba, Ricky's brother. "That was a big thing for our team."

The biggest thing, of course, is the team came together despite the many contrasts. Or perhaps all the differences created the correct dynamic.

"We all got along," said junior tackle Don Yannessa.

"We were there for a reason, to play football and to get an education," said Jackson, a junior who was a junior college transfer.

There were a mere 42 members of the 1960 New Mexico State football team. Some schools had that many assigned to holding blocking bags. This made depth a big thing. Woodson had greater depth than numbers seem to indicate. NMSU that season was a deep team because in what was a semi-one platoon era, with rules limiting while not prohibiting substitution, the ability of a number of players to handle multiple responsibilities provided much greater flexibility than might be imagined.

Kelly and Sims, along with linemen such as Witt and Yannessa, went both ways. Atkins was as good as it gets in the secondary when required there even though Woodson liked to give him a breather when the Aggies were on defense. Alba, a stalwart on defense, knew his way around the quarterback position.

The growth of the staff Woodson talked about before the Sun Bowl was not an empty promise. Tom Moulton remained line coach. Paul Alley replaced Noah Allen early in the year to coach the ends. As the season approached, Howard White was added as defensive backfield coach and defacto defensive coordinator, at least during practice. Woodson was pretty much a one-man band during games.

White, the new guy on the block, full of vim and vigor, delighted in prodding the defense to harass the offense during practice, telling his players, "It makes the offense better on Saturday." Woodson was not always happy to see his pride and joy, the offense, struggle. He made this clear by barking at White in practice, to the delight of the defensive players, who were orphans on a Woodson team. To be clear, they were not delighted their coach was getting dressed down on the field in front of them. They delighted in getting under Woodson's skin by stopping his offense.

White came from Riverside Junior College in the Southern California city by the same name. He was well acquainted with Atkins and Gaiters as Riverside JC and Santa Ana JC, the school they came from, were in the same conference. His All-American star at Riverside was none other than 220-pound linebacker-fullback Jackson.

A point for future reference was made in the *1960 Football Press Book*. The Woodson biography reads: "A complete overhaul of the athletic program at New Mexico State was needed and the road ahead appeared to be a long one. With the administration solidly behind him, Woodson began the task."

The "Prospects" section starts with this declaration: "It still doesn't sound right to the ear, but New Mexico State University appears to have another football powerhouse in the making for 1960."

These are the words of Dick Mullins, now NMSU sports information director. He could reference the past from experience, having been sports editor of *The Round Up* as an Aggie undergraduate.

"Enthusiasm is at a peak, as well it might be," he continued. "Twenty-one of the 27 lettermen are returning, including seven of the first 11."

It began with an international encounter

The season opened against the University of Mexico, formally the Universidad Nacional Autonoma de Mexico, the National Autonomous University of Mexico, located in Mexico City. It was labeled a hands-across-the-border game.

Usually, NMSU was the smaller, scrappy team, David taking on Goliath with shoulder pads and helmets rather than a slingshot. In this case, Mexico was the undersized team, with only one player in the starting lineup weighing more than 200 pounds. Left tackle Hugo Malanco was listed at 213 pounds. The lightweight of the team was 148-pound right halfback Alejandro Villalobos.

The international aspect of this game was underscored by the presence of the Cuidad Juarez municipal president, which is equivalent to a mayor north of the border. He brought a mariachi band with him to add some spice to the festivities.

The game was played on September 10, a week before most college teams had their first games, prompting a small convention of coaches to converge in Las Cruces. Texas Western's Ben Collins, Tulsa's Earl Presley and Trinity's W.C. McElhannon took advantage of NMSU's early start to scout the Aggies. Since the University of New Mexico was scheduled to play both Mexico and New Mexico State, Lobos coach Bill Weeks also was there with Ken Blue, Bob Peterson, Rod Rust and Reece Smith, the former Artesia High coach, from his staff to evaluate and understand each team.

The Pumas, known for their wide-open brand of offense, never got rolling even though it was reported that Woodson was careful to keep much of his playbook closed. He had no reason to help future opponents. New Mexico State still thumped Mexico, 41-0, to extend the winning streak from the end of the 1959 season to five in a row.

While Woodson may have kept specific plays under wraps, it was not possible for him to hide his basic game plan for the season: Give the ball to Gaiters, give the ball to Gaiters, give the ball to Atkins, give the ball to Gaiters, give the ball to Atkins. Oh, you think you can creep up to the line of scrimmage to jam Gaiters and Atkins? As soon as you do that, Johnson will throw the football.

Gaiters carried 17 times for 191 yards, an average of 11.2 yards a carry against Mexico. He scored two touchdowns.

Atkins carried 14 times for 144 yards, an average of 10.3 yards. He scored one touchdown.

Johnson completed 13 of 21 passes for 203 yards and two touchdowns, both to Kelly, who had five catches for 69 yards.

Atkins had 41 yards on his single catch. He also had one punt return for 10 yards. This gave him 195 all-purpose yards.

Gaiters got the Aggies rolling with a 25-yard touchdown run midway into the first quarter. An interception by Alba on the 40, which he retuned to the 19, was squandered when Atkins fumbled on the 12. A few minutes later, another misplay, this time a clipping penalty, wiped out a 34-yard Gaiters touchdown run. The

Aggies took a collective deep breath and reclaimed the yardage, this time with shorter gains, Gaiters eventually scoring on a 10-yard run.

To say Mexico threatened at the start of the second quarter would be an understatement. The Pumas advanced to the Aggie 1-yard line before fumbling. Along with this drive, Mexico was able to keep New Mexico State on its heels by reaching back to the Jim Thorpe era and utilizing the quick kick to drive the ball into Aggie territory. The Pumas hung on in a scoreless second quarter.

The Aggies began to pull away with a 13-yard Johnson-to-Kelly touchdown pass in the third quarter. Late in the quarter, Mexico mounted another drive, advancing the ball until NMSU took over on its own 19. From there, the Aggies drove 81 yards to score on the first play of the fourth quarter, the score coming on another pass from Johnson to Kelly, this one for 24 yards.

Another fumble, this one recovered by sophomore guard Shamburg, set the scene for a 31-yard touchdown drive with Gonzalez scoring on a 1-yard drive. The final score was on an electrifying 86-yard run by Atkins. Kelly and guard J.W. Witt pitched in with blocks as he wove his way to end zone.

Why at Tulsa two years in a row?

One of Warren Woodson's goals when he took over the New Mexico State University football program was to improve the schedule. His reasons were not complicated — better opposition would mean more recognition, which would mean he could entice better players to Las Cruces along with building attendance and the financial support that comes when you move up the college football ladder. Plus it could be a payday, as frequently is the case these days when the big guys pay big bucks to beat up on the little guys.

One problem with this big picture game plan. To get bigger, better teams on your schedule you have to play on the road. The results tend to be ugly, as they were in 1961 when NMSU went to Wisconsin and lost, 69-13. An extreme example came in 2013 when the Aggies had three paydays in four games at the start of the season, playing at Texas, Minnesota and UCLA. Predictably, they lost by big scores, 56-7, 44-21 and 59-13. That's getting outscored, 159-41.

Tulsa was a classic example on one level. Both games of the 1959-1960 NMSU-Tulsa series were played in Tulsa. The scores presented another story. The first game was a heartbreaker for the Aggies. They lost, 28-27. One difference from the standard little-guy-comes-with-hat-in-hand story. The Golden Hurricane did not play several levels above the Aggies. Fact is, they were not even a notch above the Aggies, as they discovered in 1960 during the rematch in the self-proclaimed "Oil Capitol of the World" (a claim several Texas cities may wish to dispute).

Coaches in later years, from George Allen (Rams, Redskins) to Pete Carroll (USC, Seahawks), and no doubt coaches in the 1960s and earlier, preached the importance of creating an edge in turnovers. New Mexico State proved the point for a

AGGIE MAJORETTES — No wonder the Aggies played so hard in '60, with such beauties as the girls above cheering them on. Aggie majorettes last year were, left to right, front: Mary Mayfield of Las Cruces and Joan McElroy of Van Horn, Tex.; rear: Jo Ann Joy of Alamogordo, Elsie Hartog of Carlsbad and Susan Nellis of Haviland, Kan.

NMSU Yearbook photo

second week in a row in a 38-18 victory over Tulsa. Or, as the *Sun-News* declared in its Sunday headline, "Aggies Stomp Tulsa 38-18."

With Gaiters, Atkins and Johnson to contend with, it is doubtful the Golden Hurricane spent much if any time focused on Doug Veazey, a junior cornerback. They should have because he was someone they needed to avoid. At least they should have avoided throwing the football in his direction. Veazey led the Aggie defense with two interceptions and a fumble recovery. And he was not alone in the secondary.

There were occasions in 1960 when, due to the peculiar rules of the day, Johnson played safety. Granted he played deep. "Woodson did not want the ball thrown over me," he said.

Tulsa was one of those games when Johnson stayed on the field with the defensive unit. Yes, Tulsa threw at him. It was a decision the Golden Hurricane regretted. He had an interception. So did Sims. That was one for the book. It is not often a quarterback or an end has an interception. It is even less often when both do it in the same game.

The NMSU offense also did its share of stomping, led by Gaiters. He was a workhorse for the Aggies, carrying 21 times for 104 yards as he scored four touchdowns on runs of 13, 3 and 2 yards and 1 foot. Not to be forgotten is Sims returned his interception 64 yards to the 3, after which Gaiters scored.

Records and reports from this era and area can be sketchy. *Sun-News* sports editor Abe Perilman told his readers Gaiters also scored a two-point conversion. NMSU's hand-written official "Summary of Football Game Statistics" sheet does not credit him with those two points. Rather, it has Johnson passing to Sims for 2. As hard as it is here to question a newspaper report, the fact is Gaiters would lead the nation in scoring with 145 points on 23 touchdowns and seven PAT kicks, each worth a point. That is documented. Using the "Summary of Football Game Statistics" sheets, his totals for the season come to 23 TDs and seven PATs for 145 points.

Interestingly, later in the game story Perilman does credit Johnson-to-Sims for the two-point PAT pass. So there you have it.

The remaining scoring was provided by Atkins on a 31-yard pass play from Johnson, a 32-yard field goal and two PAT kicks by Kelly and a PAT kick by Pete Smolanovich,

It was another relatively low-key game for Atkins with two carries for 31 yards, two catches for 24 yards and a 16-yard kickoff return. It would be a mistake to claim that, when not running or catching, he could take time off as a decoy. When he did not have the ball tucked firmly in his arm, he was expected to, and did, block.

A new development, as Woodson began to expand the offense, that would cause nightmares for coaches preparing to face New Mexico State was the incorporation of the fullback into the running game. Jackson carried nine times for 32 yards and Gonzalez twice for 19, providing an additional 51 yards on the ground.

Also hats off to the defense for getting to the quarterback. Gaiters, not to be left behind on defense by Atkins and Johnson, was credited with a stop of quarterback Jerry Keeling early in the game on a two-point conversion try. One Golden Hurricane drive ended when Yannessa crushed Keeling. The backup quarterback, who is not identified in the report of the game, was sacked by Langford.

Trinity was a small school with large ambitions

Trinity University, located in San Antonio, had Texas-sized ambitions despite an enrollment of 1,700. As recently as 1954, the Tigers had posted a 9-0 season. They were 8-1 in 1953. The '54 schedule was a Lone Star State mapmaker's delight. They handled, among others, Southwest Texas, East Texas State, Texas Western, West Texas State and North Texas. Now they were seeking to move up the college football ladder by adding Southwest Conference member Texas A&M to their schedule.

Trinity would face Texas A&M a week after it played New Mexico State. Texas A&M would only defeat Trinity by a 14-0 count. That was impressive if you were evaluating the game from the standpoint of the Tigers.

There was nothing impressive about Trinity against NMSU. Someone at the *Sun-News* could not help himself and repeated the "stomp" headline with "Aggies Stomp Trinity Tigers 45-0." Well, that's what happened as they extended their winning streaks to three for the season and seven over two seasons.

Sun-News sports editor Perilman took to calling Atkins and Gaiters the "Gold-dust Twins" after this game, a nickname used previously for such sports luminaries as golfers Byron Nelson and Harold "Jug" McSpaden and Australian tennis stars Lew Hoad and Ken Rosewall. The Tigers would not argue the claim the Aggie duo belonged in such elevated company.

On this particular Saturday night in Texas, Gaiters carried 18 times for 96 yards, scoring two touchdowns. He now had 48 points for the season, placing him No. 1 in the nation in scoring. Although this was the first time in three games he did not pass the 100-yard mark rushing, he still was second in the nation in rushing.

Atkins, as was his custom, was all over the place. He carried the ball four times for 73 yards, an eye-catching 18.3 yards per carry average. He added 17 yards with three receptions, one a touchdown throw of 6 yards, along with 18 more yards on a kickoff return.

Johnson did his part with yet another steady, efficient performance, completing 10 of 18 passes for 139 yards and the TD pass to Atkins. He also did a little fancy stepping, gaining 39 yards rushing against 9 minus yards for a positive 30 on the final tally. In the air, Johnson and Alba (2 of 3 for 29 yards and 1 TD) spread the ball around, throwing to six Aggies, three times each to Atkins, Sims and Royce Cassell and once to Jackson, Smolanovich and Ron Logback.

Sims gobbled up 81 yards with his catches, a very impressive 27.0 yards per catch. Logback joined Atkins with a TD catch, from 16 yards out. The game opened with a 79-yard Aggie scoring drive, the highlights of which were a 42-yard pass to Sims and another to him for 19 yards, after which Gaiters powered in from the 3.

Trinity quarterback Charles Patterson completed 2 of 11 passes for 33 yards. He had more "completions" to Aggies, throwing three interceptions. Backup QB Harris Connell threw one pass. It was an interception. Four interceptions. That's clear. Morris Hodgson with two, Frank Cusenza and Kelly with one each are credited with picks in the *Sun-News*. Turn to the Trinity section in NMSU's "Summary of Football Game Statistics" and everything lines up with Patterson tagged with three interceptions and Connell with one. The problem comes when you check out the NMSU stats and find Hodgson with those two interceptions, Cusenza and Kelly each with one AND Smolanovich also with one. That's five interceptions.

The best guess is Trinity threw an interception late in the game, perhaps when reporters were fighting deadlines, possibly even after they filed their stories (it happens), Smolanovich was the thief, he got credit on the NMSU sheet and someone neglected to account for the play on the Trinity sheet. Ah, yes, fun and games as we try to sort things out 55 or so years later.

Before administering the stomping, NMSU did have to survive an early nervous moment. After Gaiters' score late in the first quarter, Trinity's Tommy Ezell quieted the Memorial Stadium crowd with a 61-yard kickoff return. Who did he think he was, Pervis Atkins? They had taken to calling Atkins "Afterburner." This time it was Ezell activating his own afterburner for added thrust. Plus he had excellent blocking on the run, which always helps. The fact that he did not score helped the Aggies. The Tigers advanced to the 4-yard line before the NMSU defense stiffened and stopped them on four downs.

The second New Mexico State touchdown, this one early in the second quarter, followed pretty much the same script as No. 1. Johnson threw 20 yards downfield to Sims.

The throw was high. No problem. Sims went up and snagged it. Moments later, Gaiters went over left tackle to score from the 9.

Kelly was another Aggie who was all over the field. He, Langford and Floyd Strickland ganged up on Patterson, tackling him in the end zone to put two more points on the board with a safety.

Johnson threw his TD pass to Atkins with 29 seconds remaining in the first half to give NMSU a comfortable 21-0 lead. The ill-advised Patterson-to-Kelly combination got the Aggies rolling again in the third quarter. Kelly scored on a 22-yard interception return. Kelly was not done for the night, any more than the Aggies were not finished tormenting Patterson. After a Patterson fumble gave them possession, and they were unable to move the ball, Kelly kicked a 43-yard field goal, two yards short of the Border Conference record. The final two scores were provided in the fourth quarter by backups, Charles Pettes on an 11-yard run and Alba passing to Logback for 16 yards.

UNM rivalry week

After a week off for some good old R&R, rest and recuperation, a bye in football lingo, it was time to hit the road to Albuquerque to play traditional rival University of New Mexico.

Bill Weeks was the new Lobos coach, replacing Marv Levy, a surprise hire by Cal at the age of 35 after going 14-6 in two years at UNM. Levy was early in a career that would take him to four Super Bowls with the Buffalo Bills, all losses. The Lobos began the season with a 77-6 win over Mexico, on paper a much more impressive win than New Mexico State's 41-0 conquest of the Pumas. UNM then lost, 13-3 at Wyoming and 33-17 at Texas Western.

You know what they say. Records go out the window when rivals play.

A state of New Mexico record sports event crowd of 26,673 at the new 30,000-capacity University Stadium saw Johnson, Atkins and Gaiters light up the Albuquerque skies in NMSU's 34-0 victory. The *Albuquerque Journal* wrote, "Officials from the University of New Mexico and Albuquerque also scored sort of a triumph as the traffic, in complete opposition to the opening game, moved smoothly into the new University Stadium." Clearly, it was a matter of priorities.

Johnson threw for two touchdowns as he completed 13 of 21 passes for 161 yards. His favorite target in this game was Sims, who had 7 catches, 86 yards, 1 touchdown.

Atkins' basic statistics are pedestrian. He carried five times for 26 yards and caught 3 passes for 45 yards. There was more. Much more.

For those who had spent two weeks wondering what happened to his afterburner, he turned it on for plenty of boost in this game, scoring on a 65-yard punt return.

Atkins also scored on a 25-yard pass from Johnson and a 2-yard run. Plus he had an interception with a 23-yard return.

Not to be overshadowed by his partner, Gaiters blasted off for a 71-yard touchdown run. He gained 161 yards, amazingly matching Johnson's passing yards, on 16 running plays, an average of 10.1 yards a carry.

Quite obviously, the defense did more than simply show up. This was the third shutout in four games for the Aggies, earning themselves a "dead-end street" sobriquet from a press box poet.

After a scoreless first quarter, NMSU established order with a pair of touchdowns, the first a 4-yard pass to Sims. Then came Atkins with his scintillating TD run. Three Lobos appeared to have him cornered on the Aggies 47, only to have him break free and do his afterburner thing to the end zone.

A late and long drive by the Lobos at the end of the first half came up short. They drove from their own 23 to the 2, where the Aggies stiffened and denied them access to the end zone.

Gaiters found his own afterburner in the third quarter with his 71-yard touchdown run. Woodson switched Gaiters and Atkins in the fourth quarter, playing Atkins at tailback and Gaiters at wingback. This provided Atkins with some work at the position he played in 1959 when he led the nation in rushing and scoring. If needed there, as he was in '59, he would be acquainted with the timing and feel of the position.

The move also provided coaches of future opponents with something extra to think about and to prepare for when they played NMSU. It provided one other thing in this game. Atkins scored on that 2-yard run off right tackle on a classic Woodson wing-T power play. Or, as the *Journal*'s Russell wrote, "Atkins lugged the balloon over …" Ah, this was an era when the poets in the press box never rested. After Johnson passed to Atkins for the final touchdown, it was Gaiters who kicked the PAT.

The streaks were growing. The Aggies now had won 4 in a row this season and 8 in a row over two seasons.

Woodson looks to junior colleges

For years, the foundation of Woodson's teams were service veterans. They were older, generally more mature and obviously more accustomed to discipline than teenagers straight from high school. With the '40s and '50s history, and the flow of vets slowed to a trickle, Woodson was turning more and more to junior college transfers. His backfield featured the California duo, Atkins and Gaiters, from Santa Ana JC, and Johnson from Schreiner Institute in Texas. Sims, another Texan, out of Cisco JC, was at one end. Jackson, a third import from California, from Riverside JC, had worked his way up into a starting slot at fullback against the UNM.

The starting lineup now had Johnson at quarterback, Gaiters at tailback, Atkins at wingback and Jackson at fullback. Up front, Kelly was the left end, Strickland the left tackle, Witt the left guard, Bill Wallace or Carl Covington the center, Ken

Hays the right guard, Zivkovich the right tackle and Sims the right end. Yannessa was working his way up the ladder to become the starting right tackle.

McMurry jumped to early lead

The next victim for the Aggies would be McMurry, yet another Texas school, this one from Abilene, with big ambitions and a small enrollment, this one 1,100. The coach was Grant Teaff, in his first year as a head coach in a career that would take him from McMurry after six years, to Texas Tech, where he was an assistant coach for three years, to Angelo State for three more years and, finally, to Woodson's alma mater Baylor for 21 seasons to round out 30 years as a college head coach.

Despite NMSU's 43-11 win over McMurry in 1959, there was concern in the Aggie camp because the Indians, in a series that went back to 1947, had won seven times, losing only four.

An Associated Press dispatch this week would lead with the fact that Gaiters, by virtue of his 161 yards against the University of New Mexico, was leading the nation in rushing with 522 yards. Utah State's Tom Larscheid, a name to remember, was running second with 519 yards. NMSU led the nation in rushing with an average of 422.5 yards a game.

The *Sun-News*' Perilman took on the world, or at least the college football world as he saw it, in his "Behind the pipe" column on Thursday before the McMurry game. Beginning with "Let's talk some more about national ratings and raters," a topic his readers knew was near and dear to his heart, he complained about the lack of national attention and respect afforded the Aggies. He ended by puffing away with "All we can suggest now is for these guys to make a trip down here if they want to see the No. 1 team in the country." Close inspection indicates he was talking about the national total offense leader. He did make the point, "One wire service ranks the Aggies 20th in the nation ... while another wire service ... unranks (sic) the Aggies, who in fact, failed to get a single vote in the weekly poll." While he was not calling for the No. 1 ranking in these polls, he was pleading for more attention to be paid to NMSU.

There was no stomping and no shutout this time around. What there was for the first time in the season was nervous time at the start of a game when McMurry took a 10-0 lead. NMSU did get its act together, controlling the rest of the game for a 47-17 victory.

Gaiters continued to rumble, carrying 28 times for a net of 177 yards. Jackson got involved with a dozen carries. He gained 50 yards and scored twice in what was his coming out party. Now, along with Atkins, Gaiters, Johnson, Kelly and Sims, opposing coaches had to account with a bruising fullback. Johnson was more efficient than ever, gearing down to throw only 11 times, but completing 8 for 119 yards and a touchdown.

Atkins only carried once, just getting back to the line of scrimmage. He caught 4 passes for 81 yards and a touchdown. Oh, and he did have one electrifying play, an Atkins signature play, if you will, a 77-yard kickoff return for a touchdown.

It was a cold night courtesy of a "cold norther" and New Mexico State was just as cold early in the game. The shaky start was the result of three lost fumbles, turning the tables on the Aggies after they profited big time at the start of the season by victimizing the opposition. By the end of the game, the case of butterfingers led to seven NMSU fumbles, six of which McMurry recovered. NMSU countered with two interceptions, both by Alba.

Two of the early fumbles led to a McMurry touchdown and field goal. That would have been two touchdowns had Allan Sepkowitz not tackled McMurry's Don Davis, who was returning a punt, from behind on the Aggie 16.

The Aggies found their offense in the second quarter, taking the lead on a 4-yard touchdown run by Gaiters and a 7-yard touchdown run by Jackson. The lead was not permanent. McMurry had one more touchdown, taking a 17-14 lead before NMSU's defense got into the swing of things. Johnson connected with Atkins on a 40-yard scoring pass on the final play of the first half to reclaim the lead at 20-17.

Atkins set the tone on the opening kickoff of the second half, gathering the ball on the Aggie 23 and rambling the 77 yards to score. Moments later, Alba intercepted and Gaiters punched the ball over from the 1. Gaiters would score again, this time from the 3, before the quarter was over. A McMurry fumble led to the final touchdown, a run from the 7 by Jackson.

Props for the defense

Down in El Paso, *Times* sports editor Chuck Whitlock, in his "Here's How" column, set the scene for Wichita University's (now Wichita State) upcoming visit to neighboring Las Cruces.

For those who think the 48 miles between El Paso and Las Cruces is too much to consider them neighbors, understand we're talking about the wide-open spaces of the American Southwest.

Calling the game a "lulu," a term not frequently associated with football, Whitlock wrote, "The Aggies are a known quality. They are power and speed and offense plus, and they also have an outstanding defense."

Members of the NMSU defense had to be cheering. Far too often they were ignored as accolades poured in for Atkins, Gaiters and Johnson. Even today they will tell you Atkins, Gaiters and Johnson deserved every word of praise they received. At the same time, it is nice to be noticed.

"Wichita University could be the best team the Aggies have played thus far this year," Whitlock continued. "Hank Foldberg, the former Army and Texas star, is the Shockers' head coach and has done a fine job. Last Saturday they defeated Cincinnati 28-6 and are in the driver's seat in the Missouri Valley Conference."

Foldberg played at Texas A&M for a year and then for three years on Coach Red Blaik's Army powerhouses, where he was a consensus All-American end in 1946. He was not on the losing side in a game at West Point. Those teams were 9-0 in 1944, 9-0 in 1945 and had 9-0-1 in 1946, the tie coming in a scoreless game against Notre Dame in Yankee Stadium. Wichita's win over Cincinnati was by a 25-8 score.

Twin terrors such as Atkins and Gaiters had a familiar ring to Foldberg. His Army teammates were 1945 Heisman Trophy winner Doc Blanchard and 1946 Heisman winner Glenn Davis.

NMSU assistant coach Alley scouted Wichita in Cincinnati. This left Woodson with two assistants, Moulton and White, for the McMurry game. In previous seasons, if an assistant was on the road scouting, Woodson and one assistant handled the duties on game day.

Alley's report on the Shockers: "They're big, strong and aggressive. They're great opportunists. Against Cincinnati they capitalized on every error. The Aggies can't expect to make mistakes against this club and win."

Excitement was running high for the game, which was homecoming at New Mexico State. Bleachers were brought in to expand Memorial Stadium's capacity from 7,500 to 10,000 or close to 11,000, depending on which report you elect to believe. Attendance, originally guesstimated at 9,000, was officially listed at 8,616, making it the largest crowd of the season thus far for a home game.

Do you remember the Glenn Campbell song "Wichita Lineman," called by *Rolling Stone* magazine the first existential country song? It actually is Jimmy Webb's song. He wrote it. Another actually — Web was in Washita County in rural Oklahoma when he was inspired to write the song. Washita became Wichita because Wichita sounded better.

Well, pre-game expectations of a donnybrook between these big, bad Wichita linemen and New Mexico State turned out to be empty. Instead, it was another big win for the Aggies, 40-8, win number six of the season, stretching the winning streak to 10 over two seasons.

For the second week in a row, the Aggies created some anxiety when they fell behind early, this time 8-0. It was shock the Shockers the rest of the way.

First, the shock to the Aggies, another jittery start caused by another lost fumble. Wichita won the pre-game coin toss, elected to receive, did so, got nowhere and punted. Atkins received. Atkins fumbled on the 12. "… had the ball jarred from his hands," the *Sun-News*' Perilman wrote. As Coach Alley projected, Wichita took advantage of the opportunity and scored.

Have no fear, Gaiters is here. Battering Bob added three more touchdowns while gaining 107 yards on 20 carries. He continued to lead the nation in scoring and yards gained on the ground. Atkins was asked to carry a little more of the rushing load this week, carrying 11 times for 91 yards.

Jackson pitched in with nine carries for 73 yards, and two touchdowns. That's Atkins averaging 8.3 yards a carry, Jackson 8.1 and Gaiters 5.4. These Witchita linemen were not up for the challenge.

Johnson was, well, Johnson, throwing 20 times, completing 13 for 151 yards and one touchdown. Atkins caught the TD pass, a 21 yarder, one of four catches for him, as he added 53 yards to his total for the game. He also returned two punts for 8 yards and one kickoff for 24. His all-purpose yardage for the game was 176. In addition, he averaged 34.7 yards on three punts. After throwing two interceptions the previous week, Alba returned the favor by intercepting two passes this time around. Cassell was Johnson's primary target with five catches, matching Atkins' total of 53 yards.

Opportunistic football? New Mexico State could play that game too. Kelly recovered a Wichita fumble on the Shocker 40. Three plays later, Jackson rambled off left tackle to score from the 28. Next Wichita series, next fumble, this time the recovery by Hodgson. On the Shocker 46. Five plays later, Jackson scored again, this time from the 9.

Was Wichita wondering about this Gaiters guy they had heard so much about during the days leading up to the game? As his numbers indicate, they would find out about him soon enough. Boom. Boom. Boom. Gaiters scored from the 2. Gaiters scored from the 1. Gaiters scored from the 14. Johnson-to-Atkins, set up by a Gonzalez interception, capped the touchdowns for the game.

ASU/taking control of the Border Conference

New Mexico State had completed what in 1960 was called the intersectional portion of its schedule. This tag has since been discarded and it now would be said the Aggies were 6-0 in the non-conference portion of their season. It was on to the Border Conference, which included Arizona, Arizona State, Texas Western, Hardin-Simmons and West Texas State along with NMSU as members. The schedule was short, only four games for the Aggies. Arizona, demonstrating the Border was more a loose confederation than a conference, elected not to play New Mexico State. Another example of how loose things were along the border, the Aggies had to go on the road to play at ASU, West Texas and Hardin-Simmons before finally closing the season with a home conference game against Texas Western.

The NMSU-ASU game generated something of a media frenzy. It went beyond New Mexico, Arizona and the southwestern corner of Texas when *Sports Illustrated* magazine jumped in, sending a reporter to spend time in Las Cruces to gather background material and then write about the game. In Phoenix, a headline in *The Arizona Republic* declared, "Border Title On Line." The *Phoenix Gazette* announced "Aggies Hold Big Edge," deciding they were favored by two touchdowns. The hometown *Sun-News* got right to the point with "Border Conference Football Title Hinges On NMSU-Sun Devil Game."

The cherry on top of this football season sundae was the weekly Associated Press poll. Iowa was the No. 1 team in the country for the second week in a row, receiving 34 first-place votes and 458 points, followed by Mississippi (9/395) and Syracuse (5/355). Then came Navy, Missouri, Minnesota, Baylor, Ohio State, Washington and Michigan State to complete the top 10. Also receiving votes in order were Tennessee, Arkansas, Rice and Auburn, followed by, each with eight points, Purdue, Duke and Oregon State and then New Mexico State with five points followed by Kansas with two. Breaking into the top 20 was welcome news to the Aggies. It was very big news in Las Cruces.

Frank Kush was the Arizona State coach. At 31, he already was in his third year running the show for the Sun Devils. He had paid early dividends on ASU's decision to go with someone so young, posting records of 7-3 and 10-1 in his first two seasons at the helm. He won the 1959 Border Conference championship. In all, he would go 176-54-1 there. In an embarrassment of riches compared to NMSU, Kush had four assistants, a freshman coach and two graduate assistants, giving him a staff of seven compared to Woodson's three.

Arizona State ran what it called a multiple winged-T. Sounds a lot like the Woodson wing-T, which could and did morph into multiple configurations. The Sun Devils were 5-1. It is hard to believe they were 14-point underdogs when you consider they had wins against Washington State, 24-21, and BYU, 31 0, and their lone loss was 12-7 to San Jose State, a 34-20 winner earlier in the season over Stanford.

This was without dispute the biggest, most important football game in New Mexico State University history. At least it would be for two months until the Sun

Bowl against Utah State. But there would have been no Sun Bowl and no win over Utah State had NMSU not taken care of business on October 29, 1960 in the Phoenix suburb of Tempe.

No one took care of business in this 27-24 NMSU win better than Atkins. He had 213 all-purpose yards – 121 yards on kickoff returns, 8 yards receiving and 84 yards rushing. He averaged 34 yards on three punts. Whatever was required, Atkins was up to the task. Gaiters gained 81 yards on 18 carries and scored a touchdown. Johnson was 7-for-14 for 61 yards and one touchdown passing.

One account had Langford doing every bit as much damage as his headliner offensive teammates. He was credited with 13 unassisted tackles and 12 assists. You do not need to crank up the computer and feed proprietary software into it to provide an analytics study to figure out he made an impact by being in on 25 tackles. He also had a very important interception.

It was, to put it mildly, a wild game, beginning with Arizona State driving 92 yards on 19 plays, "methodically grinding it out," the *Sun-News*' Perilman reported, to take a 7-0 lead. Dornel Nelson scored the touchdown on a run from the 1.

New Mexico State countered with a drive of its own, 75 yards on 14 plays. Gaiters contributed 49 of those yards, including the final 4 to score and make it 7-7.

Zivkovich recovered a Sun Devil fumble on the final play of the first quarter. This set the scene in the second quarter for the Aggies to go ahead, 14-7, on a 1-yard run by Jackson.

The lead did not last until halftime. Sticking with their methodical game plan, the Sun Devils marched 75 yards in 11 plays, Ray Young running from the 3 to score. This made it 14-14 at the break.

Arizona State eased ahead, for the second time, on a 20-yard field goal by Nolan Jones. Field goals being something of an oddity in those years, Perilman felt it necessary to write that Jones had kicked his fourth straight field goal that season. The Sun Devils were back in charge, barely,17-14, as the third quarter ended.

Another ASU drive, this one 77 yards in 13 plays with Nelson scoring the touchdown from the 12 and the Sun Devils now were definitely in charge, 24-14.

Had Gaiters cast a shadow over Atkins?

Those who said so ignored the fact that Atkins ran with the ball, caught the ball, was a decoy, was a blocker, returned punts, returned kickoffs and played defense along with occasionally punting and kicking. He also threw a pass against Arizona State. It was not complete. Still, Woodson thought enough of him to give it a try.

Arizona State's seemingly comfortable lead became much less so following the kickoff to the 2.

With apologies for a repeat performance with a shortened version from the prologue, here's what happened next:

Atkins gathers the ball on his own two-yard line, starts up the west sidelines and heads north. He's on the 20 … the 25 … the 40. Key blocks seem to be working …

FIRST IN HISTORY — One of the benefits of an undefeated football season for the Aggies involved the winning of the Border Conference title, outright, for the first time in history. In 1938 NMSU tied for the football title with the University of New Mexico. Shown receiving the Border Conference trophy above are, left to right, Quarterback Charley Johnson and Tackle Lou Zivkovich, co-captains of the '60 squad. Presenting the trophy is G. R. Hamiel, faculty representative to the Border Conference from NMSU.

NMSU Yearbook photo

One last lunging Sun Devil misses. Perv breezes past … on the west side as he sprints into the end zone. Now it's 24-20 … miss the extra point kick. Atkins made that 98-yard trip much faster than it takes to read this description.

Lots of NMSU excitement. A small group of students and Las Cruces town people there to root for the Aggies went wild. But ASU still was on top by four points with time running short in the fourth quarter. Worse yet, the Sun Devils were once again on the march, driving to the 2, where they fumbled, Sepkowitz recovering for the Aggies on the 4.

Fortunately for NMSU, Atkins had something left in his tank, not enough to go all the way, but enough to crank out a 71-yard run to the Sun Devil 26.

Nail-biting time as the clock went tick-tick-tick toward the end of the game. It went like this: Johnson, of all people, gained four. Atkins lost two. Perhaps his gas gauge now pointed to empty. Gaiters could only get the two back. Fourth-and-six. Had Gonzalez not missed the PAT after the last touchdown, a field goal attempt would have been a possibility. Now it was not an option. Johnson to Kelly for 17 yards. First down on the 5. Gonzalez for 2. Jackson no gain. Johnson to Kelly in the end zone from the 3. Touchdown. Kelly, Smolanovich, Atkins and Gaiters had kicked PATs during the season. Gonzalez lined up once again to kick the PAT. He was Woodson's designated PAT kicker for this game, and Woodson was not one to change his mind once it was made up. Gonzalez now successfully kicked his third PAT of the game and season. NMSU 27, ASU 24.

The game clock read 3:51. No time for a methodical, time-consuming drive. The thing is, Kush was not exactly pass happy with his two junior quarterbacks, Joe Zuger and Ron Cosner. Zuger was 4-of-6 for 39 yards with an interception. Cosner was perfect. But he had only thrown three times, for 37 yards. With the game on the line, Cosner ruined his own day and ended ASU's hope with a pass Langford intercepted.

Now there was 1:17 on the clock. NMSU had possession. The long bus ride home was not going to seem all that long to the Aggies.

Atkins only promoted himself on the field

New Mexico State University football officially was on the map. The nation had taken notice. Not only were the Aggies ranked, not only had *Sports Illustrated*, the beacon of national sports notoriety in this pre-ESPN era, taken notice, Atkins was dubbed Associated Press Back of the Week. That was a very big deal. A week earlier, the recognition had gone to Navy's Joe Bellino, who was on his way to winning the Heisman Trophy.

Never one to pat himself on the back, Atkins told AP, "It's a wonderful feeling to be named Back of the Week. I can't express it. But I'm much happier that we pulled that game (out) and I'm just grateful what I did helped when it did. I was just playing football to help the team." Floyd Mayweather, LeBron James and others of their self-congratulatory ilk would scoff at such a humble response.

West Texas State letdown time?

From the beginning of time, athletes and their coaches have talked about the need to prevent getting too high or too low. NMSU had been as high as is possible in the win against Arizona State as well as during the days following the win. Now came the West Texas State Buffaloes. You did not have to have a doomsday mentality to ask the question. Would the Aggies lose a little, or even a lot, of their edge in Canyon, Texas?

Although he could not have appreciated having to play three Border Conference opponents in a row, worse yet having to play each game on the road, one quirk in the schedule had to please Woodson. There was a second bye on the schedule, and it came between Arizona State and West Texas State games. Woodson could use the time to bring his players down to earth, to reclaim their attention with some of his infamous harsh words and equally harsh workouts.

Perilman, sounding more like a coach than a columnist, identified West Texas a "a formidable foe." Not to worry, he assured readers, because "… New Mexico State's head coach, Warren Woodson, is not taking the battle with the Buffs lightly. He said line coach Tom Moulton scouted the West Texas-Trinity game, which the Buffs won 28-0, last Saturday and came away impressed with the power, speed and improvement of the club."

Think about what must have been going through the minds of the players when Woodson and Moulton talked about West Texas and all that power, speed and improvement. Let's see, they had defeated the Buffaloes handily, 35-13, in 1959. They had dispatched Trinity, 45-0, four games ago. Not a lot to get fired up or worried about protecting their 7-0 1960 streak and 11-0 run going back to the end of 1959. Add to this that West Texas had a 3-5 record.

"We're facing a real tough opponent which will be pointing for us," Woodson insisted. "They have come up with a well-rounded ball club that passes well and runs well. We'll have to be at our peak if we intend to keep that streak alive."

Did he pull the speech out of a binder he saved from a class on coaching at Springfield College?

This was Woodson's way of telling his players the other guys were going to show up, that they would not hand the game to New Mexico State simply because of all those complimentary newspaper clippings they were sending home to their families.

The scouting report from the Arizona State game had to stress the importance of containing Atkins on kickoff returns and on those relatively rare occasions when he ran from scrimmage. As the Sun Devils discovered, his explosive running ability could turn a game around.

Remember, Gaiters had gained only 81 yards in Tempe.

So what did Woodson do at West Texas in the 35-15 New Mexico State victory?

He went back to the basic football approach he had used for most of the season — give the ball to Gaiters. On this occasion, he gave the ball to his workhorse tailback 19 times. Gaiters responded with 155 yards. He did lose one yard for a net of 154 yards, an average of 8.1 yards a carry as he scored two touchdowns. This put him over the 1,000 yard mark at 1,071 yards.

As also was part of Woodson's basic football approach, it was not all Gaiters. Jackson carried 12 times for 67 yards, Atkins carried nine times for 56 yards and even Johnson carried nine times for 40 yards and a touchdown. Gonzalez slipped in one additional carry for four yards. That's 31 carries for 167 yards for a 5.4 average by the supporting cast and 50-231-6.4 when you

Pervis Atkin shakes hands with a West Texas State "Buffaloes" player before the 1960 Homecoming game. The Aggies won 35-13. (NMSU Yearbook photo)

add in Gaiters. Do you want to talk about formidable? Then you talk about the NMSU running game. Yannessa had to be smiling. He now was listed as the starting right tackle, making him a contributor to that formidable running game along with tackle Strickland, guards Witt and Hays, and Wallace or Covington at center.

West Texas coach Joe Kerbel, in his first season with the Buffaloes, was a captain in the inactive Marine Reserve. This was an occasion when a former Marine enlisted man – that would be Atkins – had the final word. He caught four passes for 102 yards, a sparkling average of 25.5 yards a catch. Sims caught five for 76, an average of 15.2 yards a catch. Obviously, Johnson had another impressive performance, completing 13 of 24 passes for 205 yards and two touchdowns

NMSU had a fairly even scoring line, going 7-7-7 in the first three quarters and 14 in the fourth quarter when West Texas clearly was worn down. The Aggies were on the Buffalo 7 when the game ended.

Gaiters scored the first touchdown on a 2-yard run. Johnson scored his first college running touchdown in the second quarter on a 3-yard run. Johnson threw a 7-yard TD pass to Kelly to give the Aggies a 21-7 lead. West Texas came back to make it 21-15.

Before anyone had much time to worry, or to get excited, depending on your rooting interests, Johnson threw an 11-yard touchdown pass to Atkins to restore order. Gaiters nailed the West Texas coffin shut with a 20-yard TD run. For the second game in a row, a Langford interception, this one with 30 seconds remaining, was the final Aggie highlight. New Mexico State now was 8-0 for the season and 12-0 over two seasons.

Atkins All-American

The NEA people – the Newspaper Enterprise Association – got it right when they announced their All-American team. Atkins was selected to the first team along with Pitt end Mike Ditka, Yannessa's Aliquippa (Pa.) High teammate, Navy's Bellino and such celebrated players as Ohio State fullback Bob Ferguson, along with linemen Merlin Olsen of Utah State, Bob Lilly of TCU and E.J. Holub of Texas Tech. The Aggies would learn all about Olsen in about a month and a half.

An All-American first-team selection was a historic first for New Mexico State. It now is a first-and-only because the Aggies are still waiting for their second All-American first-team selection to come along.

Syracuse halfback Ernie Davis, the 1961 Heisman winner, was on the second team, a clear indication word of Atkins and NMSU had spread. Gaiters was NEA honorable mention, placing the Aggies in rarified atmosphere with multiple players on the team. Texas and Baylor had three players so honored. UCLA, Rice, Minnesota, Texas Tech, Utah State each had two. That was it, eight teams, including NMSU, with multiple All-America players. The little guys were receiving recognition usually reserved for the big guys.

On Tuesday, November 15, curious college football fans picked up their newspapers to discover Missouri was No. 1 in the country in the prestigious Associated Press poll with 34 of 49 first place votes and 457 points in a system in which reporters voted on a 10-to-1 scale. Next came Iowa (7/379), Mississippi (5/362), Minnesota (1/328) and Washington (1/268) to complete the top five. The rest of the top ten were Duke (205), Arkansas (173), Navy (156), Auburn (1,104) and Ohio State (56).

Others receiving votes were UCLA (23), Michigan State (21), Purdue (12), Yale (9), Rice (9), New Mexico State (9), Syracuse (9), Alabama (8), Oregon (7), Florida (7), Utah State (6), Michigan (4), Army (3), Baylor (2), Texas (2), Kansas (1) and Tennessee (1).

Are you scratching your head over Auburn ranked down the line at No. 9 with 104 points receiving a No. 1 vote?

That's how it works. It's just a matter of opinion. In this case, one reporter decided 48 other reporters did not get it.

Should undefeated New Mexico State University have its nose out of joint because not only was it ranked no higher than tied for 14th, it was listed third among the four teams in that slot?

Or should the Aggies be smiling because Alabama, Oregon, Florida, Utah State, Michigan, Army, Baylor, Texas, Kansas and Tennessee were below them?

At the end of the day, it was just a matter of opinion.

OK, it also was a matter of pride.

Hardin-Simmons coach on way to 0-20 record

You can be assured Hardin-Simmons University coach Howard McChesney did not need help from NEA or AP to know about Atkins, Gaiters and their co-conspirators. While this was his first season running the Cowboy program, he had been a member of previous coach Sammy Baugh's staff for three years.

This was not the finest hour for Hardin-Simmons, where Woodson had been 11-0 in 1946. The Cowboys were winless when NMSU arrived in Abilene. They would remain so, by a 40-3 count, prompting the *Sun-News* to pull out the familiar and always welcome "Aggies Stomp" headline once again. It was not a barnburner. Rather, it was the Cowboy barn that was burning. One thing about McChesney's teams during his two-year tenure, they were consistent. They lost. And lost. And lost some more. They played 20 times. They lost 20 times. That's it, McChesney had a career record of an ignominious 0-20.

The Aggies now were nine and 13, they had nine wins in as many games this season and 13 in a row. Only New Mexico State and Yale, playing a pristine Ivy League schedule, were undefeated college football teams.

This time around, Johnson led the way with some deep strikes, completing 15 of 27 passes for 273 yards and a 6-yard touchdown. He connected five times to Kelly for 108 yards, an average of 21.6 yards, and the touchdown. Atkins caught

Football season, pompoms, and cheerleaders yells . . . Anxiety before the game, celebration after . . . An invitation to play in the New Year's Day Sun Bowl game, with a 28-8 victory over North Texas State . . . For the basketball team another winning season leading to the Border Conference Championship . . . Close calls to the track team where a matter of inches means so much . . . The spring season bringing forth the inning men . . . The Aggie baseball team . . . Tennis and golf triumphs keeping the Aggie name active in the sports pages . . . A newly organized gymnastics team to represent the school . . . For the women, a new gymnasium . . .

three for 73 yards, an average of 24.3 yards.

Johnson also completed three to Sims (36 yards, 12.0 average), three more to Gonzalez (30, 10.0) and one (7) to sophomore wingback Dave Thompson. On one of his catches, Gonzalez flipped a lateral to Zivkovich, who lumbered for an additional 19 yards.

Atkins accounted for 166 yards, the 73 receiving, 72 on a punt return and 21 rushing. Gaiters gobbled up 122 yards rushing on 17 carries, a healthy 7.2 average. He ran for three touchdowns. Hodgson, one of the ball hawks in the defensive backfield, had an interception.

Somewhat amazingly, given the state of Hardin-Simmons football, the Aggies were back to their bad habit of falling behind at the start. What happened was the Cowboys received the opening kickoff and, with quarterback Harold Stephens completing six passes in a row, marched to the NMSU 14, where, finally, they stalled when Stephens did not complete a pass on third down. From there, with the ball placed on the 20, Fletcher Fields kicked a field goal and they took a 3-0 lead.

Hardin-Simmons fans did not have long to rejoice. A five-play, 63-yard drive put NMSU on the scoreboard. The big play of the drive was a 48-yard Gaiters run to the 10. The way today's coaches operate, he would go directly to the bench to rest after using up 48 yards of energy. Woodson had no such compassion, or fear he might be overworking a healthy young man, which is why Gaiters carried on the next two plays, the first for no gain, which certainly would prompt a modern coach to rest him. Woodson would grin, or smirk, depending on his mood, about this approach. Gaiters scored on his second carry.

Gaiters scored again, on the third play of the second quarter, this time from five yards out. Hodgson's interception, coupled with his 30-yard return, accounted for the second touchdown. The score was a comfortable 20-0 at halftime.

Was the lead too comfortable? NMSU had matching goose eggs with Hardin-Simmons in the scoreless third quarter. The Aggies got rolling again in the fourth quarter with three touchdowns. Gaiters scored on another 5-yard run. Atkins turned anticlimactic into exciting with a 72-yard punt return for a touchdown. Kelly closed the scoring with his 6-yard TD catch. Three big plays in the quarter involved Johnson, 22 and 18-yard passes to Kelly, and a 45-yard pass to Atkins.

The decision to award the Heisman Trophy to Navy's Bellino was not applauded in El Paso. *Times* sports editor-columnist Chuck Whitlock begged to differ with popular opinion on this matter. He was all for Atkins, who finished ninth in the voting, writing, "For our money, he is the greatest single back we have seen in 15 years of covering college football. Quite frankly, he got our vote for the Heisman Award." Whitlock was not the Lone Ranger with this view. He was joined by 24 other voters wo believed Atkins deserved to win the coveted trophy.

There were smiles in Los Angeles, then the home of the NFL's Rams. They had made Atkins what was then called a future draft pick on November 30, 1959. He was the 30th player selected, in the third round.

The Denver Broncos of the American Football League, blissfully moving ahead in its first season, made Gaiters the first player selected in the 1961 AFL draft, which was held November 13, 1960.

The other rivalry

The final game of the New Mexico State schedule was against the Aggies' second rival. It might be called Rivalry Week 2.0 today. The University of New Mexico-NMSU rivalry was natural for schools inhabiting the same state. The Texas Western-NMSU rivalry was just as natural. The two schools are located 40 miles apart. One headline compared Aggies-Miners to Army-Navy. Texas Western, now UTEP for the University of Texas at El Paso, provided a high mark in Woodson's inaugural 1958 NMSU season when the Aggies eked out a 17-16 victory. The Miners provided a low spot in 1959 when they overcame a two-touchdown deficit to stun the Aggies, 20-15.

This time around, in the words of the *Sun-News*' Perilman, "The Aggie high scoring machine showed signs of a long season's wear but generated enough momentum to score a 27-15 victory …"

It was a game in which Gaiters earned a right to ask, "What's this honorable mention All-American stuff?" Ever the workhorse, he carried 23 times for 145 yards, a solid 6.3 average per carry, and two touchdowns to cement his national rushing and scoring titles. And ever the jack of all trades, Atkins gained 85 yards on a mere seven carries, 24 on one reception, 33 with two punt returns and a final 37 with two kickoff returns for 179 all-purpose yards. He also made three of three PAT kicks. Jackson, quietly coming into his own, carried 14 times and gained 82 yards.

Johnson completed 7 of 21 passes for 105 yards and one touchdown. Johnson was not an All-American. He did not receive Heisman votes. He did not receive the attention that comes with leading the nation in rushing and scoring. But his steady, efficient game, accurate arm and intelligence would serve him well in the NFL, where he played with distinction for 15 years, nine with the Cardinals, then of St. Louis, two with the Houston Oilers and four with the Denver Broncos.

Texas Western received the opening kickoff and immediately drove down field to take a 7-0 lead. NMSU followed with a drive of its own, Gaiters scoring from the 5. A failed two-point conversion, Woodson was going for the jugular early, left the Miners ahead, 7-6.

NMSU took over in the second quarter. Hodgson had started things rolling late in the first quarter when he recovered a fumble. Seconds into the second quarter, Jackson scored from the 3. The Aggies drove 68 yards for their second touchdown of the quarter, a 14-yard Johnson-to-Sims pass.

They might have broken the game wide open before intermission, in part courtesy of another Hodgsen fumble recovery. It did not happen because Johnson lost a fumble, and his two touchdown passes, each to Atkins, were nullified by backfield in motion and offside penalties.

A Gaiters run from the 9, culminating a 13-play, 81-yard drive provided insurance points. Texas Western showed some life with a touchdown early in the fourth quarter. That was it for the scoring. While the Aggie offense produced no more points, the defense shut the Miners out the rest of the way, and New Mexico State University ended the season with a 10-game winning streak, the Border Conference championship and the nation's best 14-game run over two seasons. It was Woodson's sixth undefeated team, following one at Texarkana Junior College, two at Arkansas State Teachers and two at Hardin-Simmons.

1960 Aggie Leaders

Rushing

Player	TCB	Gain	Lost	Net	Avg
Gaiters	197	1,351	13	1338	6.8
Atkins	65	624	13	611	9.4
Jackson	85	402	2	400	4.7

Passing

Player	PA	PC	Int	TD	Yd
Johnson	199	109	6	13	1,511

Total Offense

Player	Plays	Rush	Pass	Total Yards
Johnson	262	123	1,511	1,634
Gaiters	197	1,338	0	1,338
Atkins	68	611	0	611

Receiving

Player	No.	Yd	TDs
Sims	30	415	2
Atkins	26	468	6
Kelly	25	321	5
Cassell	14	148	0

Scoring

Player	TD	PAT	(2 pt) PAT	FG	Total
Gaiters	23	7	0	0	145
Atkins	12	6	1	0	80
Kelly	6	11	0	2	53
Jackson	6	0	0	0	36

CHAPTER TWELVE
Sun Bowl 1960

When he was in the dugout with the Dodgers, Hall of Fame manager Tommy Lasorda would, in his bombastic style, remind his players of "the fruits of victory." A fruits of victory highlight for a college football team is a bowl game.

There were dreams the football gods would smile on New Mexico State University and that, as an undefeated team in the Southwest, the good folks in Dallas would shine a light on them and ask them to play in the Cotton Bowl.

There could be no bigger or better fruit for the Aggies.

Warren Woodson, the old Texan, knew better. Where Lasorda was a dreamer and a major-league talker, Woodson was a plain-speaking realist. He knew thinking NMSU would be invited to the Cotton Bowl would be a waste of optimism, which is why it was no surprise then when, immediately following the win over Texas Western, he announced the Aggies and their 10-0 record would return to the Sun Bowl.

The opposition on December 31 would be Utah State, a big, bruising team anchored by junior tackle Merlin Olsen, a future inductee into the college and pro football Halls of Fame who recently had been named All-American, an honor he would win again in 1961. The Aggies would send two blockers after him all afternoon and do everything they could think of short of roping him, none of which slowed him very much.

Clearly, Utah State was a formidable opponent in this Aggies versus Aggies matchup. No matter, New Mexico State University capped its undefeated season with a 20-13 victory.

LINE ACTION — Above is an example of the rough line play which was a feature of the 1960 Sun Bowl game which the Aggies won over Utah State, 20-13. This particular play was a pass, and you'll notice the Aggies have succeeded in forcing the heavier Utags to go up and around rather than through. The Aggie line, coached by Tom Moulton, played one of its finest games of the year against Utah State, a club which ranked nationally in defense and considered its line among the best in the West.

NMSU Yearbook photo

Numbers game

As for national statistics lists, NMSU's list of accomplishments in 1960 was indeed impressive and obviously a concern for Utah State.

√ Gaiters was first nationally in rushing — 1,338 yards. He carried 197 times, averaging 6.79 yards a carry, which is benevolently rounded off to 6.8 in the NMSU *Football Media Guide*.

√ Gaiters was first in scoring — 145 points on 23 touchdowns plus he kicked 7 points after touchdowns.

√ New Mexico State was first in total offense — 4,196 yards, an average of 419.6 yards a game.

√ New Mexico State was first in scoring — 37.4 points a game.

√ Johnson was first in passing efficiency — 134.1.

√ Johnson was first in yards per pass — 7.6.

√ Johnson was second in touchdown passes — 13.

√ Johnson was third in total offense --- 1,634 yards.

√ Johnson was third in passing yards — 1,511.

√ Johnson was fourth in completions — 109.

√ Johnson was sixth in passes thrown — 199.

√ Johnson was sixth in percentage of passes completed — 54.8.

√ New Mexico State was third in rushing --- 2,639 yards, an average of 263.9 yards a game.

√ Atkins was fifth in scoring --- 80 points on 12 touchdowns plus 8 PATs.

Add to this Gaiters and Atkins combining to score 225 points was an NCAA record, and Atkins' 14.7 yards all-purpose (rushing, receiving and runbacks) average per play was yet another NCAA record.

Atkins now was an All-American twice over, named first by the Newspaper Enterprise Association and then by the Associated Press. The Williamson Rating System went with Gaiters in its backfield.

Atkins, Gaiters, Johnson, Kelly and Sims were All-Border Conference selections. Guard Jim Campbell was honorable mention All-Border Conference.

When Woodson was named Coach of the Year by the American Football Coaches Association, the announcement was met with pain and anger among NMSU faithful.

The problem? Woodson was named Minor College Coach of the Year. Let's see, the Aggies were considered a major college by the NCAA and the Associated Press, but the Coaches Association, perhaps with some axes to grind, relegated them to minor status. The topper was the Coaches Assn. elevating Ohio University, not to be confused with The Ohio State University, from the NCAA's minor classification to major.

Additional season numbers of interest: Sims had 30 receptions for 415 yards and two touchdowns, Atkins 26/468/6, Kelly 25/321/5 and Cassell 14/148/0. Jackson carried for 400 yards with a 4.7 average. It is notable he lost only two yards during the season. Alba was No. 13 in the nation with five interceptions.

Return to El Paso for Utah State

Utah State, with its own impressive 9-1 record, came out of what was then the Skyline Conference, the forerunner of the current Mountain West Conference. BYU, Colorado State, Denver, Montana, New Mexico, Utah, and Wyoming were the other members of the conference. The only blemish Utah State brought to El Paso, where it opened the season with a 20-7 win over Texas Western, was a 6-0 loss at rival Utah in the final game of the season, a demonstration of how overconfidence can trip a team up, even in a rivalry game.

The Sun Bowl loomed as a classic immovable object against an unstoppable force defense game. Utah State was allowing an average of 6.5 points a game. The Utags, as area reporters identified them to avoid Aggies-Aggies confusion, allowed 65 points in 10 games. The Aggies scored more than that in back-to-back games all but once during the season. Their low-octane back-to-back games produced 62 points.

Utah State's offensive headliner was halfback Tom Larscheid. He was second to Gaiters on the national rushing list with 1,044 yards for an 8.4 average per carry.

Utah State was coached by young John Ralston, 33, in his second season as a head coach. Like Woodson, he was a lifer, just at the other end of his run. His career would take him to Stanford, where he coached two Rose Bowl teams, winning each time, to Denver in the NFL, where he crossed paths with Charley Johnson, and finally to San Jose State, where he packed it in at the close of the 1996 season at the age of 69.

All that was ahead of Ralston. At this moment, he was a bowl game rookie coach. Woodson, on the other hand was a bowl game veteran. His record depended on your source. He had coached teams to eight bowl games. But he had coached in seven bowl games. The game he missed, a loss, was Hardin-Simmons against the Second Air Force in the 1943 Sun Bowl. He was not there because he had been called to active duty in the Navy. For some unknown reason, the *2014 NCAA Football Records* book, on page 71, does not include two games he did coach, each a victory, Arkansas State Teachers in the 1937 All-American Bowl or Hardin-Simmons in the 1948 Grape Bowl.

All that mattered in 1960 was the simple fact that Woodson had a ton of experience preparing for and playing in bowl games while Ralston was doing it for the first time as a coach. He had however been on the other side of the fence, having played in two Rose Bowls, each a loss, as a linebacker at Cal.

The big news five days before the Sun Bowl came from game chairman Bob Kolliner when he announced the game would be seen on regional television in the West, including in El Paso. That was a big deal in 1960. At the same time, he said all reserved tickets to the game had been sold. Only 800 general admission tickets remained. Another big deal, in El Paso.

Charley Johnson time

Sun Bowl time turned out to be Charley Johnson time. Reggie Jackson, 14 in 1960, an All-American baseball player originally recruited to play football at Arizona State, would become known as "the straw that stirs the drink" during his time with the New York Yankees. Johnson did exactly that, stirring things up for the Aggies. He did it two years running in the Sun Bowl as he was named game MVP each year.

Early in the game, it was about Ernie Reese. He got Utah State rolling with a 52-yard punt return to the 18. Moments later, Larscheid scored from the 13 on a sweep around right end.

Johnson led NMSU back, passing from the 2 to Atkins for a touchdown. Atkins kicked the PAT to make it 7-7.

Dolph Cammilli's 11-yard sweep, this one around left end, put Utah State up, 13-7, at halftime. Lamont Miller's PAT after the first touchdown was good. This time, according to *The Round Up*, Miller was "rushed by Aggie linemen" and his kick "went astray."

Rain had left the field a mess, creating a mud bowl. Gaiters found his mud shoes on one spectacular run in the third quarter, rambling 32 yards for a touchdown. Atkins' kick gave NMSU the 14-12 lead.

In the fourth quarter, following key completions to Kelly, Atkins and Gonzalez, Johnson threw to Sims from the 7 for his second TD pass. Atkins' kick was wide.

NMSU was ahead, 20-13. While this would be the final score, the Aggies were not out of danger. Utah State could have tied the game by scoring a touchdown and kicking the PAT or going ahead with a touchdown and a two-point conversion.

As it was, Utah State, taking advantage of its bigger line, drove to the NMSU 20 playing smash mouth football. At the 20, NMSU made a bold goal line stand. This was a time when players were allowed to think for themselves and make decisions on the field as opposed to looking to the sideline for signals or even large signs with coded messages telling them what the coaches want them to do. Alba, playing safety, went to Langford, the linebacker who served as defensive quarterback. Langford had the responsibility of setting the defense. Alba suggested they switch from their regular defense to goal line to stop Utah State's power running. This was drastic because, quite obviously, they were 20 yards from the goal line. No matter, they did switch to goal line. It worked. Utah State fullback Doug Mayberry, who had been having his way, was stopped short when he tried to hammer the Aggies on a fourth-down short-yardage play.

Johnson was on top of his game, completing 18 of 26 passes with one interception. He threw for 180 yards and two touchdowns.

Kelly caught six passes for 64 yards, Sims five for 44 and Atkins three for 28. Sims and Atkins caught touchdown passes. Jackson, Gonzalez, Cassell and Thompson each caught a Johnson dart.

Gaiters was credited with 13 carries, gaining 66, including his touchdown run, losing one for a net of 65.

Atkins carried seven times for 19 yards. The big Utah State line battered him to minus nine yards, giving him a net of 10. His 69 all-purpose yards (add 23 on a kickoff return and 10 on a punt return), well below what he generally produced, also illustrates the poor condition of the field.

Utah State's linemen introduced themselves to Johnson on more than one occasion, dumping for minus 46 yards. He did gain nine yards, leaving him with a net of minus 37.

The New Mexico State University Aggies, tucked away in Las Cruces in the Mesilla Valley in southern New Mexico, a short haul from Mexico, had completed a perfect season at 11-0 to stretch the best winning streak in the nation to 15.

Etcetera

This was not the end of the football road for all the seniors. Seven went on to play professionally. The roll call:

Pervis Atkins — Los Angeles Rams, Washington Redskins, Oakland Raiders

Bob Gaiters — New York Giants, San Francisco 49ers, Denver Broncos

Bob Jackson — San Diego Chargers, Houston Oilers, Oakland Raiders

Charley Johnson — St. Louis Cardinals, Houston Oilers, Denver Broncos

Bob Kelly — Houston Oilers, Kansas City Chiefs, Cincinnati Bengals

E.A. Sims — Edmonton Eskimos and British Columbia Lions (Canadian Football League)

Lou Zivkovich — Calgary Stampeders (Canadian Football League)

Zivkovich would go on to fame in a totally unrelated area — some are likely to label it notoriety — as a *Playgirl* magazine centerfold, which led to a few acting gigs in television; he also was an escort of entertainer Mae West, the Madonna of her time.

CHAPTER THIRTEEN

Decline and Departure — 1961-1967

It was downhill the rest of the way for Warren Woodson and New Mexico State University.

As they say, the higher you climb, fly, or whatever, the greater the fall.

And did the Aggies ever fall, crash and burn.

There was excitement and great hopes for the future. The excitement could be measured in the approval for the funds to almost double the size of Memorial Stadium from 11,000 to 20,000. Thank you, Warren Woodson. Thank you, Ricky Alba, Pervis Atkins, Bob Gaiters, Jerry Gambatese, Sal Gonzalez, Charley Johnson, Bob Kelly, Clem Mancini, E.A. Sims, Jim Worrick and Lou Zivkovich. They were the seniors from the 1960 team. How well they played was etched in stone. How much they would be missed was not yet evident.

There was a solid core returning for the 1961 season, led by three new captains, linebacker Bob Langford and guards J.W. Witt and Jim Campbell.

Cover of the 1961 Media Guide in advance of the 1961 football season.

Also back were lettermen end Royce Cassell, center Carl Covington, guard Ken Hays, fullback-defensive opportunist Morris Hodgson, battering ram fullback Bob Jackson, Ron Logback moving from end to quarterback, tackle Jack Moss, halfback Charles Pettes, guard Allan Sepkowitz, guard John Shamburg, end Pete Smolanovich, guard Floyd Strickland, halfback Dave Thompson, halfback Doug Veazey, center Bill Wallace and tackle Don Yannessa.

Plus James (Preacher) Pilot and Phil Ehly, who practiced but could not play in 1960 due to NCAA transfer rules, were now available. Pilot, from Kansas, would lead the nation in rushing in 1961 and 1962. His back-to-back totals were 1,278 yards, a 6.7 yards per carry average and 1,247, 6.7. Ehly, from SMU, was a center who would become an Aggie captain.

Two more pluses were returning squad members quarterback Lonnie Carter (known in later years as Lonnie Terry) and Armando Alba, Ricky's younger brother, a halfback squad member in 1960 who would play quarterback for the next three seasons.

THEY WON'T BE BACK — The ten athletes above had a big say in the Aggies sterling 11-0 record in 1960, but they won't be back in '61, as they were all seniors. They are, left to right front: Halfback Pervis Atkins, Quarterback Charley Johnson and Halfback Bob Gaiters; rear: Quarterback Ricky Alba, End E. A. Sims, End Bob Kelly, Center Jim Worrick, Guard Clem Mancini, Tackle Jerry Gambatese and Fullback Sal Gonzalez. Not pictured is Tackle Lou Zivkovich, the 11th Aggie who will not return in '61.

(NMSU Yearbook photo)

Additional squad members adding depth were fullback Bill Birdwell, halfback Chris Cadenhead, halfback Frank Cusenza, guard Dennis Ganstine, halfback Gary Hobbs and quarterback Don Rierson.

A near tragedy during the summer can now be seen as foreshadowing what was to come. Langford was sidelined due to a life-threatening Texas oil field accident in which his face was crushed. Major surgery was required. He missed the 1961 season, beat great odds when he worked himself back into shape and was given a release to play again in 1962, only to break his arm in the second game of the season, ending his football career.

When Carter arrived from California, he was seen as the heir apparent at quarterback. A leg injury causing him to lose movement in his foot cut his career short. He and Langford point out that despite the football team having an extremely small budget, each was kept on scholarship. This is in contrast with Woodson's image as a gruff, uncaring coach.

First up in 1961 was a ho-hum game at home against Arizona State-Flagstaff, not quite five years before the name change to Northern Arizona University. It was a 56-6 victory for the Aggies.

So the conquering heroes were out there once again laying waste to all in their path.

COACH AND HIS CAPTAINS – That's Coach Warren Woodson, left, with his three captains for the Aggies during the '61 campaign. They are, left to right, Guard J.W. Witt, Guard Jim Campbell and Halfback Bob Langford. (NMSU Yearbook photo)

Or not.

The second game was at University of New Mexico. Call it the reality check to end reality checks. It was a 41-7 loss.

It was bad enough that the nation's longest winning streak of 16 games was no more. Having the streak ended by rival UNM was rubbing salt into an open wound.

From here, the Aggies muddled through the season with a disappointing 5-4-1 record. They went downhill the next two seasons with 4-6 and 3-6-1 records. Twelve wins in three seasons was only one more than the 1960 team won.

In 1964, they had a bit of a bounce-back 6-4 season.

The Aggies won 19 times during the 1959-1960 seasons. Starting in 1961, it would not be until September 18, 1965, when they had a 27-10 win at Arlington State, now the University of Texas at Arlington, that they won their 19th game since '60.

In rivalry games during those first four years after 1960, they were 1-3 against UNM and 2-2 against Texas Western.

Woodson appeared to regain his touch with those six wins in 1964. He restored order in 1965 at 8-2. Then came 7-3 and 7-2-1 records. Not 1960 Part Two, but a respectable 22-7-1 over three years. Considering the state of New Mexico State football from the departure of Jerry Hines to the arrival of Woodson, that's a very respectable record.

Also pleasing was a 3-0 record against UNM in 1965-66-67. The flip side was an 0-3 record against Texas Western as it became UTEP.

The winning was not enough to placate NMSU president Roger B. Corbett. He decided it was time for a change, and Warren B. Woodson became the former Aggie coach shortly after the end of the 1967 season.

Personality problem

Woodson's prickly personality was the bigger problem. Remember the statement in the 1960 *Football Press Book* about how the administration was "solidly behind him." His history at New Mexico State was a repeat of Arizona, and once again support evaporated.

"They forced him out," lamented Roy Gerela, a 1966-67-68 letterman defensive back-kicker who would kick for three of Chuck Noll's four Pittsburgh Steelers Super Bowl champions.

"I was disappointed," said J.W. Witt, the bell weather of the 1960 line at left guard.

"I wouldn't say anything bad about him," said Jerry Rodich, a center-linebacker in 1965, not Woodson's biggest fan as an undergraduate, who as the years have gone by can see how the positives of his coach outweighed the negatives.

Woodson's time in Tucson ended in part because his my-way-or-the-highway approach involved more than his players. The image he left behind in Las Cruces and elsewhere ranged from tough on his players to being verbally abusive. He could be dismissive with administrators, alumni and boosters. When Woodson was not having a good day, it could get ugly, as it was when he barked at an administrator that if he did his job as poorly as this fellow the school would be in trouble.

When you think about it, it was just like the Navy. President Corbett and his key administrators were on one level. They were the senior staff. The football coach, even when he served as athletic director, was not senior staff. Ignore that fact, ignore the hierarchy on campus and you'll pay the price. A World War II vet, Woodson should have understood chain of command.

It was fast and clean when Corbett, deciding enough was enough, fired Woodson three weeks after the end of the 1967 season. Officially, it was a retirement because Woodson would reach the state-mandated retirement age of 65 before the 1968 season.

Corbett lauded Woodson in a statement which read: "In a decade full of accomplishments, Warren Woodson has lifted NMSU from small-college to major national status in intercollegiate athletics." Etc., etc., etc. Blah, blah, blah.

Woodson was conspicuous by his silence. At least he was silent for about five minutes. Then he made it clear he wanted to coach again, which was his way of saying he was not leaving NMSU of his own volition. Oh, and since UNM just happened to have an opening, following the firing of Lobo coach Bill Weeks. Woodson also made it clear he definitely would be interested if the Lobos were interested in him. They were not.

The departure of Woodson was handled with ultimate kid gloves in the 1968 *Swastika*. The headline, stylishly all lower case: "woodson era ends for state squads." There was a photo of the coach standing tall. He appears to be receiving an award, which he no doubt would trade for another season coaching football.

The text in the yearbook: "Warren B. Woodson, Athletic Director and Head Football Coach, left New Mexico State University in 1967, as one of the nation's 'winningest coaches'."

Under the direction of a previous set of editors, *The Round Up* buried the hiring of Woodson. The student paper put the coach on the front page this time with two stories, one about the "retirement" and the other about the elevation of basketball coach Lou Henson to the role of athletic director while remaining basketball coach. It also was mentioned that Jim Wood, "Woodson's chief assistant," was the new football coach. So ended the golden era of New Mexico State University football.

Etcetera

This was not the end of the football road for Woodson. He moved on to Trinity University as athletic director and, in 1972, added football coach to his job description. His teams were 8-2 and 8-3.

The school pulled the football rug out from under him by eliminating football scholarships in 1974. He responded by resigning as athletic director.

SO LONG AGGIES – It may be a while before New Mexico State has three rocketeers such as the ones above. Preparing to go into orbit, which they did many times on the football field, are, left to right, Pervis Atkins, Charley Johnson and Bob Gaiters. Each of the three athletes will see action in the National Football League this fall. Atkins with the Los Angeles Rams, Johnson with the St. Louis Cardinals and Gaiters with the New York Giants. (NMSU Yearbook photo)

What Woodson did not quite do was retire from football. Sal Gonzalez, who played for him at Arizona and NMSU, had become the New Mexico Highlands University coach in 1973. He asked Woodson to come and lend a hand. Woodson was happy to comply, as a hands-on consultant. When Gonzalez and Highlands parted company following the 1974 season, Woodson's coaching career was over. He closed the book on his football career as a scout for the Dallas Cowboys.

Woodson's football primer

A window through which you can view the psyche of the old coach is provided in the title of his book, *VICTORY OFFENSE*, written after he retired from Trinity University.

In 1961 Warren Woodson was chosen "Coach of the Year" along with Murray Warmath of Minnesota by the American Coaches Association. Woodson is pictured with his daughter, Dawn, 16, and his wife, Muriel. (NMSU Yearbook photo)

The book tells you about Woodson as well as about his innovative brand of football via the wing-T offense.

High school football players of that era who whiled away their time diagramming plays during class saw Woodson's offense as a revelation No doubt

Woodson made an editorial decision to go with all capital letters in the title to make sure his message was clear — you play football to win.

The subtitle is "A Complete Football Coaching Manual."

For those who pay attention to minute details, the full title is "Victory Offense With a 'T' Formation." Victory Offense is, as said, all caps and in large, bold type. "With a 'T' Formation" is much, much smaller type. Placing "T" in quotes is an indication the old coach was decidedly old school.

Sorry, coaches, the 163-page mimeographed manual, originally priced at $12.50, is not available. That is it is not available unless you can run down someone who has the book, perhaps the son or grandson of an old high school coach in Texas, where the offense was very popular following Woodson's success at Hardin-Simmons. Or maybe you can find an aging Aggie who has it.

That's just part one of your assignment. Part two is talking the owner into copying it for you.

It takes talent to win football games, to achieve, as Woodson wrote, victory. There was an abundance of talent at NMSU in 1960. As players who have been on star-studded teams that did not reach expected goals can tell you, it takes more than hyperbolic clippings to reach those goals. A winning system as well as a winning philosophy also are required. "Victory Offense" points the way.

To the amazement of some of Woodson's former players, primarily those who toiled on the defensive side of the ball, he did devote part of the book to such matters as the Oklahoma 5-2 defense as well as 4-5, 6-2 and 4-3 defenses.

The fact that the bulk of the space was devoted to offensive football is what Woodson players expect. When he did write about defense it often was in the context of how to defeat a specific defense with his multifaceted wing-T offense.

Aggie lettermen gather for a group photo in 1961. (NMSU Yearbook photo)

He explained many small points, such as quarterback fundamentals — "As the center snaps the ball into the palm of the right hand of the quarterback, the left hand of the quarterback snaps shut on the ball and grasps the ball on the left side and beneath the ball."

There are chapters on The Winning Attitude, Physical Conditioning and Team Organization. All of this comes before he gets into the Xs and Os of the game, complete with diagrams on who lines up where.

Woodson's "formula for success," as he wrote it, included "five basic offensive mistakes we should avoid if we plan to win."

His list in his a-to-e order:
  a. Never fumble
  b. Never have a kick blocked
  c. Never have a pass intercepted
  d. Never miss a blocking assignment
  e. Never get a penalty

Woodson's prescription for winning also included:

• "There is no easy way to win a football game. It is a battle all the way, and no team can win unless each man is willing to pay the full price for victory."

• "Football cannot be played well by loafing, lazy men."

This is Warren Woodson football. It was undefeated New Mexico State University football in 1960.

CHAPTER FOURTEEN

The Sanctions

Era Rentfrow was seen as something of a Mother Teresa at New Mexico State University, a well-respected lady, an institution on campus going back to her freshman year of 1915 when Woodrow Wilson was President of the United States and Clarence Russell guided the Aggies to a 3-1 football record.

Fast forward to 1962. Seven presidents later, John F. Kennedy resides in the White House. With apologies to a previous president, Teddy Roosevelt, here comes the NCAA waving a very big stick in the form of a three-year probation complete with bowl and television bans. According to the announcement from the NCAA, "The council cited New Mexico State for admitting seven football players, none identified, without meeting the university's regular entrance requirements."

As the New Mexico State registrar, this put Miss Rentfrow as well as Warren Woodson in the crosshairs of the NCAA, prompting calls of foul from the Aggies. Her supporters could not believe she would allow a football coach to compromise her values. That was not her nature, they insisted, citing her history.

There was and remains a considerable amount of confusion, as frequently is the case when the NCAA is involved. Special admissions above and beyond athletics were and remain common around the country. Some schools may have been slicker than others in crafting the wording of their documents to provide loopholes through which legacy students (children of alumni, generally wealthy alumni) and other candidates for enrollment with ties to donors or otherwise well-connected people and, yes, athletes could be eased into the student body. Once enrolled, they presumably were on their own in class.

Special admit students who could not handle the academic load, or simply declined to do so, found themselves former students. There is evidence this was the case at NMSU with football players, just as it was the case within the general student body.

The NCAA announcement also cited "an offer for illegal financial assistance to a football player."

The official NCAA proclamation, dated January 11, 1962, cited the NCAA Committee of Infractions as the investigating body reporting to the NCAA Council, which studied the "findings" and ruled several student-athletes (no number given in the NCAA document) "were not admitted to the university in accordance with the regular published entrance requirements ... a member of the coaching staff offered a prospective student-athlete financial assistance ... the coaching staff recruited and offered financial assistance to at least two student-athletes enrolled in other collegiate institutions without contacting the appropriate athletic officials of the institution …"

Woodson emphasized in *The Round Up* published on January 12, 1962 that it was an offer, not a payment. He also said the coach was told it would not happen. NMSU football players from that time say those in need of a little cash had access to part-time jobs. They took advantage of this access, they say. One job they cite as being available was collecting garbage for the city of Las Cruces. Such jobs were not violations of NCAA rules.

It eventually came to be known that the coach in question was Noah Allen. He soon became a former NMSU coach.

NMSU President Corbett protested the NCAA "findings," insisting the Aggies were innocent of what, when you get down to it, WOULD HAVE BEEN educational fraud.

The NCAA has a history in such matters. When it goes hunting, many call them witch hunts, and gets its claws into a school (pardon the mixed metaphors), a school does not squirm free.

The Round Up reported on May 4 that Corbett had appealed the probation, claiming "it contained at least 18 errors of a substantive nature," that "the burden of proof is placed on the accused" and in the charge of seven athletes not meeting regular entrance requirements "all except one of the students were admitted entirely in accordance with university rules regarding admissions."

The formal appeal sent to the NCAA points to incomplete transcripts provided to NMSU and, basically, charges the NCAA with a rush to judgment. The charge of not contacting officials at schools from which athletes transferred was based on the interpretation of an obscure rule by the NCAA. The Aggies were not raiding other four-year schools for players, as the charge implied. Rather, they had contacted junior college athletes without first contacting officials at the junior colleges. NMSU pointed to the words "Collegiate Institution" in the appropriate section of the rules and argued that junior colleges were not members of the NCAA and therefore there was no reason or history to think such contact was required. The NCAA was twisting a rule to justify the verdict. Once NMSU was unceremoniously disposed of, the NCAA quickly rewrote the rule to make it clear it did not cover junior college athletes.

The NCAA rejected the appeal. In an interview with *The Round Up*, also appearing on May 4, NCAA executive secretary Walter Byers disagreed with the 18 errors claim. He talked about the admission of two track athletes and he insisted six athletes who did not meet standards had been admitted to NMSU.

The Aggies served their sentence, the football program unraveled, Woodson began to rebuild, to retool, to set his house in order. Then, President Corbett's patience running thin, Woodson was fired, and the real unraveling of NMSU football commenced. On the outside looking in, it appears big-time sanctions were imposed for at best small-time infractions. That's what happens when one person or institution is judge, jury and executioner, as is the case with the all-powerful NCAA.

There are a number of ways to look at the NCAA process. Most are bad. NCAA officials point out they do not have subpoena power. They say they are doing the best they can in difficult situations. Explanation or excuse, their process smacks of McCarthyism. It is not constituted to produce fair, equal or just penalties.

In the case of New Mexico State, supporters of the Aggies assumed false accusations were filed. Some believed the false accusations came from the University to the North, aka the University of New Mexico. Further, it was and remains the belief of many that, when dealing with the notorious NCAA police, if you cannot prove without a shadow of their doubt that you are not guilty they will penalize you to the extent their law allows and possibly even beyond.

Sound like an out-of-control inquisition? Many observers feel that way. Those who study the NCAA closely accuse it of running an inconsistent judgment system, one minute handing out extremely lenient sentences for seemingly major violations and the next coming down strong for lesser violations.

At the end of the day, be it at the end of the day in 1961, 1981, 2011 or today, all the secrecy of the process creates mistrust and a feeling justice is not served.

CHAPTER FIFTEEN

The Rest of the Way — 1968-2014

Enter "The Curse of Warren Woodson."

Don't forget, this is New Mexico, the Land of Flying Saucers. Alleged flying saucers? Flying imaginations? Hmmm.

Well, Las Cruces is not Roswell. But . . .

All that is known for sure is New Mexico State University football has gone from bad to worse since the now long-ago firing of Warren Woodson. This opens the door to "The Curse of Warren Woodson," referred to by not only long-suffering followers of the program but also by the people who put together the seemingly endless rivers of information on Wikipedia.

As of the close of the 2014 season, in the 47 years since Woodson was summarily dismissed as coach and athletic director, NMSU has employed Jim Wood, Jim Bradley, Gil Krueger, Fred Zechman, Mike Knoll, Jim Hess, Tony Samuel, Hal Mumme, DeWayne Walker and Doug Martin to coach the football team. Each, unfortunately, has been unsuccessful in the effort to repeat or even come close to the Woodson magic.

Wood was promoted directly from Woodson's staff, having been hired from Allan Hancock Junior College in Santa Maria, California. Obviously, the administrators had their fingers crossed that Woodson's football acumen but not his personality had rubbed off on Wood.

Bradley, a Las Cruces High product, was a star safety as an NMSU undergraduate who put in enough time at running back to rip off a 90-yard run in Albuquerque at UNM in 1954. That was and remains two school records, both as a long run and a long run for a touchdown. Preacher Pilot matched Bradley with a 9-yard touchdown run in 1963 at Trinity. Like a number of former Aggies, Bradley became a high school coach. He was extremely successful at Las Cruces Mayfield High, winning a New Mexico state championship as he put together a 55-22-6 there. Some New Mexico sources cite his record as 52-55-6 or 52-26-6. This happens because records back when he was starting as a high school coach are sketchy. A typo or two in a yearbook or a newspaper can throw everything and everyone off. The best available information points to 55-22-6 pre-NMSU.

Bradley's jump from Mayfield directly to the head job at NMSU was yet another attempt to recreate Jerry Hines, who made the successful jump from Las Cruces High to the Aggies.

Following his run at NMSU, Bradley returned to high school coaching with renewed success, winning two more state championships with Roswell High (hmmm) and an additional four back at Mayfield. On top of this, he went to the championship game eight more times, once during his first run at Mayfield, four times with Roswell and three more times back at Mayfield. That's an impressive 15 trips to the New Mexico state high school championship football games. Bradley was inducted into the NMSU Hall of Fame in 2004. He retired from coaching in 2005. He died in Las Lcruces on August 12 2015 at the age of 82.

Krueger was a change of pace. He was a successful college coach, albeit on the Division II level, where he won a national championship at Northern Michigan.

Zechman came to Las Cruces from Columbus, Ohio, where he was an Ohio State assistant.

Knoll was yet another hire with no experience as a head coach. He had been an assistant, previously at NMSU and just prior to his return as head man with 1983 national champion Miami.

Hess came from Stephen F. Austin, where he posted a 47-30-2 record, including 10-3 his last season there. His claim to fame with the Aggies would be a 43-9 win over Cal State Fullerton in the final game of the 1990 season, ending what at that time was the longest losing streak in the country at 0-27.

Samuel had been defensive end coach at Nebraska. His NMSU moment of glory was a 35-7 win in 1999 over old rival Arizona State, then ranked No. 22 in the country. You know some old Aggies were smiling that weekend.

Mumme, a pass happy coach who had been fired by Kentucky, was hired away from Southeastern Louisiana. Like Woodson, he had a genuine track record, starting with 24-11 at Iowa Wesleyan and 40-17-1 at Valdosta State. From there it was much less impressive – 20-26 at Kentucky and 12-11 at Southestern Louisiana.

Walker came directly from UCLA, where he was defensive coordinator. The Bruins had just passed him over for the top job to hire Rick Neuheisel. Previously, he was with Pete Carroll at USC.

Martin's resume included a stint as Kent State's head coach from 2004 to 2010. His record was 29-53. He was NMSU's offensive coordinator in 2011 before bouncing to Boston College in the same position, returning to the Aggies, presumably with his eyes wide open, to become head coach in 2013.

The combined record for these coaches at NMSU, take a deep breath and exhale ever so slowly — 154-373-3. The individual breakdown: Wood (21-30-1), Bradley (23-31-1), Krueger (17-37-1), Zechman (8-25), Knoll (4-40), Hess (22-55), Samuel (34-57), Mumme (11-38), Walker (10-40) and Martin (4-20).

That's an average of 3.27659574468 wins a season and an average of 7.93617021276 losses a season.

That's 10 coaches in 47 seasons, which averages 4.7 seasons per coach. Samuel lasted the longest – eight seasons. Martin does not count as the shortest at two seasons because, as this book goes to print, he is on the job in his third season working to turn things around. The short-timer "honor" goes to Zechman – three seasons.

There have been only four winning seasons since the end of the Woodson era. Krueger did it in 1978, his first year on the job, with a 6-5 record. Jim Hess did it in 1992 with another 6-5 record. Samuel, Mr. NMSU Longevity, did it twice at 6-5 in 1999 and 7-5 in 2002.

That's 6-5 three times and 7-5 as the bright spots in 47 seasons. Add up the four winning seasons and they only gave the Aggies a 25-20 record, which is not a great deal to cheer about.

Krueger's 6-5 season did produce the Missouri Valley Conference championship. The Aggies were 5-1 in conference and 1-4 out of conference that year.

There have been only three winning seasons in the last 36 years. There were 10 losing seasons in a row following Woodson's final season, the lone winning season and then 13 more losing seasons for a 1-23 winning season-losing seasons run.

Pervis Atkins was inducted into the College Football Hall of Fame.

Amazingly, by post-Woodson Aggie standards, they then had three winning records in 11 years. The current string of losing seasons stands at 12.

Yet another negative is the Aggies have not appeared in a bowl game since their 1960 high mark in the Sun Bowl. This gives them the definitely dubious distinction of having gone the most years in what is generically called the NCAA Division I, officially the Football Bowl Subdivision or FBS, without playing in a bowl game. This is especially frustrating because, unlike the Woodson era, when playing in a bowl game was only for the select few, about all a team needs to do to qualify for one of the many bowl games now is have a faint sign of breath.

The lack of stability in the NMSU football program is seen in conference affiliations over the years. The Aggies were in the Border Conference from 1932 until it ceased existing after the 1961 season. From that point it was independent, Missouri Valley Conference, independent, Pacific Coast Athletic Association, which morphed into the Big West Conference, Sun Belt Conference, Western Athletic Conference until it dropped football in 2012, independent and currently back in the Sun Belt for football only while a member of the WAC for all other sports.

There have been highlights since Woodson. However, the brightest have been attached to Woodson, either directly or indirectly. He, and by extension NMSU, was honored by induction into the College Football Hall of Fame in 1989. That, by the way, was the ultimate hold-your-nose 0-11 season for the Aggies. Pervis Atkins joined his coach in the College Football Hall of Fame in 2010, a we-do-understand-it-could-be-worse 2-10 season for the Aggies. The length of time until the Hall of Fame got around to recognizing Woodson and Atkins is a reminder as to why a small school in the desert at times is left feeling it is not part of the club.

Lack of team success does not totally shut down individual honors. NMSU does have a list of post-Woodson All-Americans – Manny Rodrigues, 1969 Central Press third team tackle; Andy Dorris,1972 Associated Press honorable mention; Hank Cook, 1973 Associated Press third team end; Karl Dean, 1974-75 Associated Press third team guard; Todd Culter, 1992 *Football News* second team tight end; Jimmy Cottrell, 2005 *Sports Illustrated* honorable mention linebacker; Chris Williams, 2006 *Sports Illustrated* honorable mention; Derrick Richardson, 2008 *Sports Illustrated* honorable mention safety; Taveon Rogers, 2011 Yahoo Sports third team and *Pro Football Weekly* honorable mention wide receiver; Austin Franklin, 2012 *Sports Illustrated* honorable mention wide receiver.

Some of the selectors are obscure. There are a lot of honorable mentions. As Lane Kiffin, the former Oakland Raiders and USC head coach who hooked up with Nick Saban to become Alabama offensive coordinator, says when faced with questions on tough issues: "It is what it is." What it is — Atkins remains the only first-team All-American in Aggie history.

The brightest of the stars during this time may well have been running back Po James, who followed in the large footsteps of Atkins, Gaiters and Pilot. James gained 1,291 yards with a 5.7 average as a freshman in 1968, setting an NCAA freshman record. He followed with seasons of 1,182 (4.6), 641 (4.8) and 771 (3.9). The manner in which his numbers declined was typical for NMSU football.

CHAPTER SIXTEEN

Yesterday, Today and Tomorrow

As many members of the 1960 New Mexico State University team as could be contacted were asked to look back to their undefeated season. Why was this team so good? Reflecting on the time in which they played, there is no "I" in their commentary.

Δ Δ Δ

Seniors —

Ricky Alba: "We were lucky to have the best skill players in the country."

Pervis Atkins: "Magic and Woodson."

Browning Yelvington: "The team stayed together and got the system down pretty good, and there is no mistaking the fact that Pervis, Bob and Charley were stars and really blossomed the last year."

Jerry Gambatese: "*The Sports Illustrated* article about the team. That article is so true." (In the 1960 *SI* story, Roy Terrell wrote that Atkins, Gaiters, Johnson and Jackson "may be the best in the country ... no one ever accused Warren Woodson of turning out either a poor football team or an uninteresting one.")

Sal Gonzalez: "Coach Woodson, the talent of team members and the willingness of everyone to work together as a team."

Charley Johnson: "WW, WW, WW, WW." He was referring, of course, to Warren Woodson.

Jim Worrick: "When Coach Woodson took over in 1958 he changed the culture. He showed us that he expected to win."

Bob Kelly: "We had a good coaching staff and some superior athletes who were willing to work hard as a team."

Clem Mancini: "We all got along. Of course, it helped to have the great backfield we had."

Allan Sepkowitz: "There was a lot of camaraderie on that team. Guys from a lot of different backgrounds meshed together."

Δ Δ Δ

Juniors —

Chris Cadenhead: "It was Coach Woodson. He had a plan. Also, he had contacts who could and would help him in recruiting."

Jim Campbell: "We had a few great players — Charley Johnson, Pervis Atkins, E.A. Sims, Bob Kelly, Bob Gaiters and Bob Jackson. I guess the rest of us supported them."

Royce Cassell: "A great group of boys maturing into a great group of men."

Carl Covington: "Woodson was a very good coach who we respected and we expected him to lead us to victory."

Frank Cusenza: "We were a family. That was a key element."

Ken Hays: "Charley's ability as a passer and the running of Gaiters and Atkins, and Woodson's offensive philosophy made for a winning combination. Woodson had the greatest offensive mind of that time."

Bob Jackson: "I think about what we did as a team. What stands out was teamwork."

Bob Langford: "I think the most important ingredient we had was the team had a lot of players like J.W. Witt, players that came from high school programs where fundamentals were taught."

Pete Smolanovich: "We had the great athletes to play with top teams. I'm talking about Atkins, Johnson, Gaiters, Sims and Kelly plus Jackson."

Don Yannessa: "Woodson put it together — the staff, the players, booster support, administration commitment, the whole nine yards."

Lou Zivkovich: "Team maturity, weak schedule."

Bill Wallace: "Coach Woodson was the primary reason. A great backfield of Charley Pervis, Gaiters, Sal Gonzalez and Bob Jackson. Blind luck played a part, of course. A weak schedule certainly played a part, although I couldn't say that we really played any pushover besides Mexico."

Δ Δ Δ

Sophomores —

Lonnie Carter-Terry: "Charley said Woodson, Woodson, Woodson and Woodson. I would add Johnson."

Dave Thompson: "Woodson, Atkins, Johnson, Langford."

Δ Δ Δ

Freshman –

Armando Alba: "It was a mixture of skill players and overachievers. The foundation was about seven players who could play for anyone."

Bill Birdwell: "A mixture of high achievers combined with high morals, winning attitudes, unity among all and superior coaching."

Gary Hobbs: "We had some very smart players. There were guys from all over the country who came together. And the coaches."

Martin looks to past to bolster future

The Magic in the Desert season goes beyond a distant memory for current Aggies coach Doug Martin. He was not born until Feb. 4, 1963, a little more than three years after the close of the undefeated 1960 season.

No matter, student of the game that he is, Martin is tuned in to what happened all those yesterdays ago as well as to how that never-to-be-forgotten team can serve as a beacon in 2015 and beyond.

Martin knows Charley Johnson, now distinguished emeritus professor in the NMSU chemical engineering and materials department Dr. Charles Johnson, and a number of the old undefeated Aggies. He knows boosters such as Charlie Rogers, a good friend of Pervis Atkins during their student years, and Hank Cook, a 1972-73 letterman and board member of the Aggie Athletic Club and Football Success Fund.

All were part of the equation when he accepted the challenge of coaching the Aggies. Martin was offensive coordinator for the Aggies in 2011, before moving to Boston College in 2012 to be offensive coordinator there, before returning in 2014 to NMSU as head coach.

"The people here have a passion for football," he said. "I knew that."

He believes that passion can be part of a winning formula.

He also believes the Magic in the Desert Aggies can be part of that formula.

"Because I had been here, I knew the potential New Mexico State has," he said. "I knew they had won before. I use it."

He uses it to pump up his players, to provide them with something tangible in terms of Aggies getting the job done more than occasionally.

"I talk to the players about winning," he said. "I tell them it has been done before here. When the old players are on campus, I have them speak to the team. I tell the players, 'These men came here and were very successful and they are dying for you to be successful. All these guys just want us to be a success.'"

About the revolving door for coaches

Coaches come. Coaches go. Such is life in college football. "You're hired to be fired," more than one coach has lamented.

This definitely has been the story for New Mexico State coaches since Warren Woodson.

The record indicates coach after coach after coach did not have whatever it takes to get the job done. But what might have happened if the right coach had been given extended time to turn things around, such as Rich Brooks at Oregon?

The situation for the Ducks for 10 years in the 1960s and 1970s was similar to the situation at NMSU for the Aggies as Jerry Frei, Dick Enright and Don Read spun in and out of Oregon's revolving door.

Enter Brooks. He had very little success, witness four two-win seasons, only semi-balanced by moderate success, five six-win seasons, during an uneventful 12-year run in which his record was 52-77-4.

The Ducks stuck with him. He rewarded them with back-to-back 8-4 seasons. Then came a 3-8, 6-6 and 5-6 dip. They still stuck with him. This time he rewarded them for their patience, delivering a 9-4 record and a trip to the Rose Bowl.

The NFL came calling. Brooks went off to coach on Sunday, leaving the program in very good shape for Mike Bellotti, Chip Kelly and now Mark Helfrich to build on his success, developing Oregon into a national power.

Might NMSU have had a Brooks and not allowed him to stick around long enough to build a solid football program?

"I've studied every coach who has gone through New Mexico State," said NMSU graduate Michael Bradley. "There have been some good coaches, some very good coaches. The difference has been an assistant coach here and there, a few players." Bradley is a qualified observer. In the nine years from 2006 to 2014, he took Mayfield High of Las Cruces to the New Mexico large-school high school football championship game. He won three state titles. The losses in 2013 and 2014 were by one and two points.

Bradley is more than a casual observer of Aggies football. He is the middle son of Jim Bradley, the NMSU coach from 1973 to 1977. Coaching football is the family business. His brothers, Jim Jr. and Gary, also followed in their father's footsteps to become high school coaches. Gary won the New Mexico state 4-A championship with Farmington High in 2013. Jim Jr. coaches in Texas.

Michael is not shy about supporting his father. No upset there.

"Obviously, he thought he could get it done," Michael said. "I always thought he could get it done. He won every other place he coached." Some will say he was a great high school coach who could not make the transition to the college level. Others will call this a simplistic response. All Jim Sr. may have needed was support and patience approaching the level Brooks received at Oregon. "He had some good teams that were just on the very edge of going above .500," Michael said.

A win or two or three more and Jim Sr. may have been retained. The same no doubt could be said about others who followed in Woodson's wake.

"He was always on the edge of having a winning record," Michael repeated. "That is the epitome of New Mexico State football. That last year was maybe a little tougher than the previous four. The newspaper was basically calling for his head. I didn't take that too darn well. It was devastating to the family when he was fired."

That obviously was not a fun time for 14-year-old Michael.

He prefers happier memories of those years.

"The great thing was being on the sidelines with my dad," Michael said. "I was either the ball boy or just hanging out with him."

Mario Moccia: "We have to take the right roads"

New Mexico State University athletic director Mario Moccia has what he calls "a vivid memory" of NMSU football.

"It was a neck-and-neck loss to Angelo State," he said.

It was a neck-and-neck loss in 1987 when Moccia was an NMSU undergraduate, and Mike Knoll was the coach.

The Aggies had an opportunity to pull one out. They had the ball on the Angelo State 6-yard line. There were 50 seconds remaining in the game. The Aggies advanced five yards and two feet in four plays.

They ran the ball. They ran the ball. They ran the ball. They ran the ball again. Four plays. It took them 41 seconds. Nine seconds remained on the clock. A dozen inches remained on the field between the ball and the end zone.

Good clock management except for one basic point. They had run out of downs.

The heartbreaking final score: Angelo State 21, NMSU 17.

The Aggies coming up short on the football field. How frustrating. How typical for NMSU when Jerry Hines or Warren Woodson is not the coach.

In this case, add embarrassing to frustration. Angelo State was a Division II team.

Moccia represents NMSU football yesterday, today and tomorrow. He was there in 1987-88 and 1988-89, a transfer from Scottsdale Community College. He was the first baseman on the baseball team, the team MVP each of his two seasons. He is there today as the new athletic director, having assumed the position on January 5, 2015. He has accepted the assignment of molding the future success of the athletic program. He understands the simple truth of his job — football is the engine that drives a college athletic program.

The results during Moccia's years as a undergraduate were typical of the post-Woodson years. NMSU was 2-9 and 1-10 for an overall 3-19 record. The Aggies were 0-7, 0-7, winless in 14 games in their conference, the Pacific Coast Athletic Association. In a real head scratcher, the lone win in 1988 was 42-29 at Kansas.

As a new student in 1987, Moccia was not yet invested in NMSU athletics. Still, he recalls the feeling on campus after the loss. "I remember everybody being deflated," he said. It now is his assignment to do some inflating.

Moccia is tuned in to boosters and former football players. He finds they are not locked in the past. Their focus, like his, is on the future. As an example, the 1960 season is not a drum they constantly beat. "It is not brought up on a regular basis," he said. "They want the program to get better. They want the focus to be put on football."

One of the problems NMSU has faced is conference affiliation as it has bounced around the country from conference to conference until landing in the Sun Belt Conference for football. The seemingly natural gathering of NMSU, UNM and UTEP in one conference has not happened.

The reality is we're a Division I member and there is no way we're going to the Autonomous Five," Moccia said.

Autonomous Five may be a new title for you. It is the politically correct term for the Power Five Conferences, the ACC, Big Ten, Big 12, Pac-12 and SEC. They have a stranglehold on the big bowl games. This which means they have a stranglehold on the big bowl money. Lacking charity in their hearts, they are not inclined to let go.

"We're in the Group of Five," Moccia said.

Call them The Rest or the On The Outside Looking In Group. They are the American Athletic Conference, Conference USA, the Mid-American Conference, the Mountain West and the Sun Belt.

"Among these conferences, there certainly is a hierarchy," Moccia said. "Two years ago, our conference, the Sun Belt, was ranked sixth among the BCS conferences. You can't be ranked any higher."

That's reality speaking. The Power Five conferences are, when you strip it all down to the essentials, a self-perpetuating monopoly. Teams on the outside might, have and will slip into their ranks. It is not going to happen for an entire conference.

Conference membership has been an on-going source of frustration for the Aggies since the Border Conference vanished after the 1961 season.

"That's always a topic," Moccia said. "What's the best conference? What makes the best sense? That's always a hot topic among our fans. When you get around to it, conference alignment is on football. It's all football. You saw what happened to the Big East. (Defections of football-playing members prompted the Big East to reinvent itself.)

"I tell people, football drives the train from the revenue and conference standpoint. We're always going to be geographically challenged."

There is only one way to get the attention of, say, the Mountain West Conference.

"It's up to football," Moccia said. "That dovetails into why supporting football is important. It is have-to. There is no option."

What would seem to dovetail is the regional grouping of NMSU, UNM and UTEP in the same conference. That has not happened. Instead, NMSU is in the Sun Belt Conference for football (the Aggies are in the WAC in all other sports), UNM is in the Mountain West Conference and UTEP is in Conference USA.

"It would make sense for us all to be in the same league," Moccia said. "What softens it is that we play each other every year."

Adding all-three-in-one-conference to the package would add to the rivalries. Plus there would be marketing advantages in such a package. But anyone who has observed college sports knows what makes sense is not always what happens.

Since it is up to football to drive the athletic program, it does come down to one question. How does NMSU drive football back to relevance?

It makes sense (there we go again, looking for things that make sense) to take a good look at Boise State, like UNM a member of the Mountain West Conference. Boise State was not on the NCAA map in 1960 when NMSU was undefeated. It was a junior college.

Boise State would seem to have the same out-of-the-way geographic handicap as New Mexico State. No problem, the Broncos made a steady climb to four-year college, NCAA Division II, NCAA Division I and even to becoming a player on the national football level while the only thing steady for the Aggies has been the lack of a similar climb. The Aggies were a comet flashing in the college football sky in 1959 and 1960, and then disappearing out of sight.

Moccia sounds primed for the challenge when Boise State is mentioned.

"There are examples all over the place," he said. "Look at Kansas State University. It had the longest losing football program in America, no fan base and it is located in Manhattan, Kansas. Then here comes Bill Snyder."

Snyder took over a team that went 0-26-1 in the previous 27 games and flipped a switch from perennial loser to perennial bowl team. He went to a bowl game in his fifth season at Kansas State. Starting with that team, K-State has gone to 16 bowl games in 18 seasons. (Snyder took a three-year "retirement" break.)

"I was at Southern Illinois," Moccia said of his previous place of employment. "They were considering dropping football. Then along came a guy from Emporia State, Jerry Kill. Three years later, they were the No. 1 (Division 1-AA, now FCS) team in the country. He took them to five straight playoff appearances. He parlayed that to Northern Illinois, where he was able to build a bowl team, and now he's at Minnesota, where he has taken a team that had been struggling with a 37-50 record in the seven seasons before his arrival to three straight bowl games."

This leads Moccia to a conclusion.

"You have to have the right coach with the right plan and, sure, you have to get a little lucky," he said. "There are tremendous examples. There are road maps. We have to take the right roads."

This leads him to yet another conclusion. It concerns Doug Martin, the current coach of the Aggies.

"When you have a situation like New Mexico State, there might be a tendency to try to flip it quick," he said. "That does not work. In my mind, you have to recruit good, quality kids and redshirt them. You win with 22-year-olds, not with 19-year-old kids. That's Doug's approach. I like it."

This is the way it is with New Mexico State University football headed into the 2015 season.

Epilogue — A Chance Meeting

Warren Woodson, Head Coach 1958-1967

As a student, I was a journalism major, and because that major was part of the English Department, I occasionally saw Prof. Tom Erhard after he joined their faculty in 1960; however, the Tom Erhard I knew better was the guy who was to become "The Voice of the Aggies," and he knew a few things about Warren Woodson. Let me explain.

From his first days on campus, Erhard began announcing all Aggie football and basketball home games on the public address system, and he said that he never missed announcing a game for more than three decades, starting in 1960. We often saw each other — particularly in the press box of Aggie Memorial Stadium. Erhard remembers meeting Woodson in the press box, where he often positioned himself, relaying his instructions to the team on the field during the game.

As Erhard told me, "I remember one of the games. It was hot in the press box — stuffy little cubbyholes with no air conditioning — and I was going into the announcing booth when Woodson came up to me and said, 'Get out of my way. I need to be here.'

"I answered, 'Well, I need to be here also.' Woodson replied, 'There's somebody here who needs to pray,' and I answered, 'I don't need to pray but I need to announce the game.' The minister accompanying Coach Woodson, and who was going to say the prayer before the game, was able to get into the next booth. It turned out that Woodson's booth was right next to mine."

Erhard recalled another tense moment during the 1961-62 basketball season when NMSU was using the Las Cruces High School gymnasium. Woodson was attending a game in his position as athletic director. Again, Erhard was there to announce the game, and he was in the crowded lobby of the building when he felt a sturdy push from behind. When he turned to confront whoever was behind him, he was face-to-face again with Woodson. Erhard remembered Woodson saying, 'I am the university athletic director, and I have a basketball game I need to watch."

As they traded dirty looks, Erhard's response was, "I am the announcer for the basketball game, and I need to be there to announce the game."

They again exchanged hostile looks and went into the gymnasium. Erhard said there was no indication Woodson recognized him, though they had shared the same press box for years. The reason for that was made clear two weeks after Woodson "retired."

Looking at the matter of Woodson's forced retirement from the university seven years later, Erhard said that he believed it was after the Aggies steamrolled over Northern Arizona University in Flagstaff, 90-0, that the coach's fate was sealed and his career at NMSU ended.

Less than two weeks after Woodson's job ended, Erhard told the story of going to Dean Peugh's Chevron station in Las Cruces to get gasoline. Peugh was one of the strongest Aggie boosters, and many of the university's faculty and staff traded at the station. As fate would have it, Woodson was at the station that day, having his car serviced.

Erhard approached him and, after a brief introduction, said, "I did your announcing. You were a superb coach." Woodson said, "Thank you," and they began talking in a conversation that lasted about 20 minutes.

Woodson surprisingly opened up as they talked. "I'm sorry you were let go," Erhard said. Woodson replied, "You know, nobody in this town ever understood me. All I did in the years I was here was concentrate on football. For example, I would bump into somebody (on campus or in town) and the only thing I had on my mind was next week's game. I didn't have time for chatting with townspeople. I had to spend every day concentrating."

Erhard remembered being fascinated at this side of the coach he considered aloof and distant. Woodson continued, "People said I was a football genius, but I wasn't a football genius. I had to concentrate on the next game. If you came up to me, you would not be important to me. I would have to answer your questions, but you were in my way."

Talking about it at a later date, Erhard said he came to believe the conversation provided insight into the mentality of the man who had such an illustrious and at the same time rocky career at NMSU.

Woodson's final comment to Erhard that day was, "If this were a week ago, I would not be talking to you." Erhard said he never forgot those last words and, at the time, Woodson's daughter, Dawn, was taking one of his English courses.

– Dan Perry, 2012

Acknowledgments

Before Dan Perry died March 9, 2013, he secured the promise from his college roommates and fellow journalism students that his dream of his book, *Magic in the Desert*, would be realized. And so, while the book is a fascinating history it also has a fascinating history. The title is from a quote Dan penned from All-American Pervis Atkins, and Dan was determined to immortalize the greatest football season ever known at New Mexico State University.

Over the years, Dan had accumulated a research archive on the events and players of the 1960 undefeated Aggies as well as maintaining contact with many members of the team. NMSU journalism professor Frank Thayer and Torrance, Calif.-based sports columnist Mike Waldner set about fulfilling the promise, joined also by Dan's lifelong friend Charlie Rogers handling many of the pre-publishing as well as post-publishing details.

The three were not alone. Mike interviewed 34 Warren Woodson NMSU players for the book, including 26 members of the undefeated 1960 team. Some more than once. Some in person. Some on the phone. Some via email. All, whether quoted or not, provided important information to help shape the final form of *Magic in the Desert*. The 1960 players are brothers Armando and Ricky Alba, Bill Birdwell, Chris Cadenhead, Jim Campbell, Lonnie Carter, Carl Covington, Frank Cusenza, Dennis Ganstine, Jerry Gambatese, Sal Gonzalez, Ken Hays, Gary Hobbs, Bob Jackson, Charley Johnson, Bob Langford, Clem Mancini, Allan Sepkowitz, Pete Smolanovich, Dave Thompson, Bill Wallace, J.W. Witt, Jim Worrick, Don Yannessa and Browning Yelvington along with redshirt Phil Ehly. In several cases wives and children of players facilitated the interviews.

A major challenge would be to invoke the excitement and promise that attended each game of the 1959 and 1960 Aggie football seasons. Mike, the seasoned *Daily Breeze* sports columnist, was the perfect professional to write the story of each game, each big play and to resurrect Dan's voice in the telling. Mike added to the research and wrote the lion's share of this Aggie sports history, weaving statistics into the clap of shoulder pads and the breathtaking passes and runs, well enough to satisfy the appetite of the most discriminating Aggie fan along with inserting human interest elements into the book..

Among those who assisted were the family and friends of Pervis Atkins (poor health prevented him from participating) and the families of the late Jack Moss and Ron Logback (he was in bad health and has since passed away). Valuable information also came from six players who preceded the 1960 team, George Mulholland, Danny Villanueva, Joe Kelly (Bob Kelly's older brother), Art Camarillo (he was at NMSU during the spring of 1960 but did not return after going home for the summer), Dick Rudzik (a 1959 player who could have but did not return for the 1960 season) and Billy Ray Locklin. More valuable information came from post-1960 Woodson players Roy Gerela and Jerry Rodich. This grew the number of Woodson players who participated directly or by proxy to 37. Las Cruces Mayfield High football coach Michael Bradley, son of Jim Bradley, who coached the Aggies during the 1973-77 seasons, also helped paint the picture of the post-Woodson era.

No acknowledgment would be complete without thanking Dan's wife Irene, who engineered his scholarship endowment to the NMSU journalism department and who offered encouragement for the book along the way.

Special notice must be given to Walt Hines, son of legendary Aggie coach Jerry Hines, for his unflagging support of the project as well as some important contributions to this history and to the inner decisions leading to Warren Woodson's hiring. As well, Chris and Kay Cadenhead must be mentioned for decades of maintaining the team network and arranging reunions. Kay has always been considered the "den mother" of the team.

Add to this list Dick Mullins (1960 NMSU sports information director), Pat Hill-Yandell (student athletic department secretary in 1960), Tyler Dunkel (assistant NMSU athletic media relations director from 2001 to 2005 when he became assistant athletic director for athletic media relations, a position he held until 2014), current coach Doug Martin and current NMSU athletic director Mario Moccia. Special thanks goes to Mike's wife Nancy, who volunteered to read and massage the very raw drafts of the manuscript as well as the final page proofs. Some of the photos were provided courtesy of New Mexico State University Archives and Special Collections Department.

Δ Δ Δ

Proceeds from *Magic in the Desert* will go to the Daniel R. Perry Endowment Scholarship, which was created in August, 2013 by Irene Perry to be awarded annually to a New Mexico State University student pursuing the news editorial emphasis in the department of Journalism and Mass Communications. Anyone interested in contributing to the Perry Endowment can do so online at giving.nmsu.edu or by mailing a check to NMSU Foundation Inc. P.O. Box 3590, Las Cruces, N.M. Information is available by emailing giftacct@nmsu.edu or calling 800-342-6678 or 575-646-6126.

Δ Δ Δ

Anyone with additional information, corrections or comments about *Magic in the Desert* can contact Mike Waldner at mwsptcol@aol.com.

Friends since childhood, Charlie Rogers and Dan Perry pose for the camera in 1944 Ft. Sumner, N.M.

(From left, below) Dan Perry, his best friend Charlie Rogers and his roommates and *Round Up* colleagues Frank Thayer and Mike Waldner. Rogers' class photo is from the 1959 Yearbook, and the other photos are from the 1962 Yearbook. (NMSU Yearbook photo)

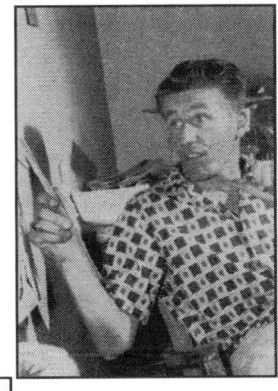

A Selection of Player Photos from 1960

E.A. Sims

Dave Thompson

J.W. Witt

Jim Worrick

Don Yannessa

Lou Zivkovich

1960 Aggie Team Members Departed as of Summer 2015

Morris Hodgson
Bob Kelly
Ralph Leonard
Ron Logback
Jack Moss
John Shamburg
E. A. Sims
Floyd Strickland
Doug Veazey

INDEX

A
Alba, Armando —xii, 82, 114, 130, 139
Alba, Ricky — xii, 64, 65, 70, 75, 81, 83, 84, 88, 92, 94, 110, 113, 114, 129, 139, 142
Alexander, Dale — 79
Allen, George —85
Allen, Marcus —61
Allen, Noah —65, 67, 79, 122
Alley, Paul —83, 93
Apodaca, Lauro —38, 39, 40, 41
Apodaca 'Hooky' —31, 39, 40, 41
Arrington, Lavar —61
Askew, Presley —35, 51, 64
Atkins, Pervis —vii, xi, xii, xiii, xiv, 19, 42, 71, 72, 73, 74, 75, 77, 78, 79, 81, 82, 83, 84, 86, 87, 88, 89, 90, 91, 92, 93, 94, 96, 97, 98, 99, 100, 101, 102, 103, 104, 105, 108, 110, 111, 113, 114, 117, 127, 128, 129, 130, 131, 139, 142

B
Badenoch, Arthur —10, 12, 13, 18
Balsamo, Tony —67
Bannister, Roger —71
Barber, Charles, M. —12, 13
Beatty, Orren —47
Bellino, Joe —98, 100, 103
Bellotti, Mike —132
Bennett, Joseph — 8
Bergman, Alfred —16
Bergman, Arthur J. —13, 16, 18
Berrier, Ann —26
Bickel, Jim —65, 70
Bickerstaff, C.R. —64, 66, 79
Bilichick, Bill —18
Birdwell, Bill — xii, 114, 130, 139
Blaik, Red —93
Blanchard, Doc —93
Blue, Ken —84
Boushelle, J. Paul —50
Boyland, Chuck —52
Bowers, Vernice —26
Bradley, Gary —132
Bradley, Jim —51, 125, 126, 132, 140
Bradley, Jim Jr. —132
Bradley, Michael —132, 140
Branson, John —34. 51
Brees, Drew —11
Bridges, Preston —79
Brokaw, Tom—75
Brooks, Rich —131, 132
Brown, Gordon —16
Brown, Mack —57
Brown, Robert 'Cap' —10, 13, 16, 18, 73
Bryan, George S. —21
Bryant, Bear —29,
Burkholder, Arthur R. —13, 17
Buvens, Margaret — 13
Byers, Walter —122

C
Cadenhead, Chris — xii, 70, 76, 79, 114, 129, 130, 139, 140
Cadenhead, Kay —140
Calabria, Tony — xii
Camilli, Dolph —110
Camarilla, Art —139
Campbell, Glenn —93
Campbell, Jim — xii, 70, 73, 75, 79, 108, 113, 115, 139, 142
Cann, Bill —40
Caranta, Irene —xv, 1,
Carlisle, Billy Joe —79
Carroll, Pete —85
Carter-Terry, Lonnie — xii, 114, 130, 139
Carruthers, Garrey —23
Cassell, Royce — xii, 70, 75, 79, 88, 94, 105, 108, 111, 113, 130, 142
Cavallo, Anthony —35, 51, 52, 53, 55, 57, 64, 65, 66, 67
Cazares, Davis —19
Cerny, Bob —75, 79
Cherry, Ed —38
Clark —22
Cline, Burton —40

INDEX

Clute, W.M. — 7, 8, 9, 10, 12, 13
Coffman, Ted R. —13, 18
Cohee, Dick—66, 70, 72
Coleman, Joseph —35, 50, 51
Collins, Ben —84
Conlan, Shane —61
Connell, Harris —88
Cook, Hank —128, 131
Corbett, Roger B. — 5, 53, 55, 57, 64, 115, 116, 122
Corley, Vaughn —35, 36, 40, 45, 46, 48, 50, 52, 55
Cormany, Charles —13
Cosner, Ron —97
Cottrell, Jimmy —128
Covington, Carl — xii, 70, 75, 79, 90, 100, 113, 130, 139
Crosby, Bing —42, 43
Cunningham, Johnny —32, 41, 43, 44
Culter, Todd —128
Curfman, Babe —35, 48
Curley Vaughman —35
Cusenza, Frank — xii, 88, 114, 130, 139

D

Davis, Don —92
Davis, Ernie —100
Davis, Glen —93
Davis, Wilton —60
Dean, Karl —128
Detterick, Bob —40
Detterick, Master —40
Ditka, Mike —100
Doherty, Ed —62
Donohue, Bob —49
Dorais, Gus —22
Dorris, Andy —128
Druxman, Jay —6
Dunkel, Tyler —140

E

Egerton, Kearney —29
Ehley, Phil —113, 114, 139

Eisenhower, Dwight D. —74
Enright, Dick —131
Erhard, Tom —137
Ezell, Tommy —88

F

Fields, Fletcher —102
Ferguson, Bob —100
Foldberg, Hank —92, 93
Folz, Mickey —64, 65
Franklin, Austin —128
Frei, Jerry —131
Fulghum, Mildred —26

G

Gaiters, Bob —vii, xii, 71, 72, 73, 74, 75, 77, 78, 79, 81, 82, 84, 85, 86, 87, 88, 89, 90, 91, 92, 93, 94, 96, 99, 100, 102, 103, 104, 105, 108, 109, 110, 111, 113, 114, 117, 128, 130, 142
Gambatese, Jerry — xii, 113, 114, 129, 139
Ganstine, Dennis — xii, 114, 139
Garrett, Chester —13
Garrett, Mike —61
Gerela, Roy —116, 140
George, Anthony 38, 39, 40
Gipp, George —16
Gonzalez, Sal — xii, 68, 73, 75, 79, 81, 85, 87, 94, 97, 99, 102, 110, 113, 114, 117, 129, 130, 139
Goodell, Roger — 10
Greely, Horace —72
Griffith, John G. —13, 15, 16, 18, 22

H

Hadley, Hiram — 8
Hagerty, Prof. — 8
Ham, Jack —61
Hamicl, G. R. 97
Hardman, Brittain —66, 68, 69
Harris —22
Hartog, Elsie —86
Hartzell, Dave —79
Hayes, Jim —51

INDEX

H (continued)
Haynes, Abner —77
Hays, Ken — xii, 68, 75, 91, 79, 100, 113, 130, 139
Hedgecoxe —22
Helfrich, Mark —132
Henson, Lou —35, 117
Hepburn, Katherine —40
Hernandez, Art —70
Herron, Bob —79
Hess, Jim —125, 126
Hill (Miss) —25
Hill-Yandell, Pat —140
Hines, Jerry — 18, 29, 30, 31, 32, 33, 34, 35, 36, 40, 41, 43, 45, 46, 48, 55, 57, 73, 115, 125, 133, 140
Hines, Walter — 10, 11, 13, 14, 18, 31, 32, 33, 34, 36, 39, 41, 55, 140
Hixon, Emmett —31, 40
Hoad, Lew —87
Hobbs, Gary —xii, 114, 130, 139
Hodgson, Morris —xii, 88, 103, 104, 113, 143
Holguin, Sam —67
Hollowell, Carl —66
Holt, Alfred —12, 13
Houlgate, Deke — 12
Howard, Jack —46, 47
Hummel (Hummell), John E. —14
Hummel (Hummell), W.G. —12, 13, 14, 15, 16

J
Jackson, Bob — xii, 81, 82, 83, 87, 88, 90, 91, 92, 94, 96, 97, 105, 108, 110, 111, 113, 129, 130, 139
Jackson, Reggie —110
James, LeBron —98
James, Po —128
Johnson, Charley —vii, xii, xiii, 64, 65, 66, 67, 68, 70, 73, 74, 75, 77, 79, 81, 84, 86, 87, 88, 89, 90, 91, 92, 94, 96, 97, 100, 102, 104, 105, 108, 109, 110, 111, 113, 114, 117, 129, 130, 131, 139, 142
Johnston, Julius —18, 35, 45, 46
Jones, Nolan —96
Joy, Jo Ann —86
Junell, Frank —38

K
Kail, Bill —79
Keeling, Jerry —87
Kelley, Louis —65, 73, 75, 79
Kelly, Bob — xii, xiii, 65, 70, 73, 75, 77, 79, 81, 82, 83, 84, 85, 87, 88, 89, 90, 91, 94, 97, 101, 103, 105, 108, 110, 111, 113, 114, 129, 130, 142, 143
Kelly, Chip —132
Kelly, Joe —64, 65, 68, 70
Kennedy, John F. —121
Kerbel, Joe —100, 139
Kiffin, Lane —128
Kill, Jerry —135
Kimbrough, Frank —58
Klein, Sonny —6
Knoll, Mike —125, 126
Kolezar, Frank —79
Kolliner, Bob —109
Krueger, Gil —125, 126, 127
Kush, Frank —95, 98
Krzyzewski, Mike —81

L
Laabs Bud —46
Ladd, Shaler —27, 28
Landin, Ben —65, 75, 79
Langford, Bob — xii, 75, 79, 81, 87, 96, 98, 100, 110, 113, 114, 115, 130, 139
Lanier, Buck —vii
Larscheid, Tom —91, 109, 110
Lasorda, Tommy —107
Leonard, Ralph — xii, 143
Levy, Marv —89
Locklin, Billy —65, 70, 71, 75, 79, 140
Logan, Fred —41, 42

INDEX

Logback, Ron — xii, 70, 76, 79, 88, 113, 139, 142, 143
Lohman —22
Lopez, Chickie —51
Lucas, Ed —79
Luppino, Art —61, 62

M

Madonna —111
Malanco, Hugo —84
Mancini, Clem — xii, 75, 79, 113, 129, 139
Manning, Payton —11
Marsh, Virgil —50
Martin, Doug —125, 126, 130, 131, 135, 140
Master, Hugo —39
Mayberry, Doug —110
Mayfield, Mary —86
Mayweather, Floyd —98
McCarrell, Gary —79
McCarty, George —35, 51
McChesney, Howard —101
McElhannon, W.C. —84
McElroy, Joan —86
McKinney, T. Burns —39
McSpaden, Harold 'Jug' —87
Mechem, Ed —36
Mechem, Jay —36
Melder, Jerry —79
Menadace, Larry —79
Miller, Lamont —11-
Miller, John O. — 10, 11, 12, 13, 14, 18, 34
Mobley, Rudy —59, 61
Moccia, Mario —132, 133, 134, 135, 140
Moss, Jack — xii, 113, 139, 143
Moulder, Maurice —35, 47, 48
Moulton, Tom —65, 67, 79, 83, 93, 98, 107
Mulholland, George —65, 70, 73, 75, 78, 139
Mullins, Dick —52, 83, 140
Mumme, Hal —125

N

Naismith, James —58
Nations, Walter —31, 40
Negrea, Sam —65, 70
Nellis, Susan —86
Nelson, Byron —87
Nelson, Dornell —96

O

Obama, Barack—75
O'Hara, Tony —79
O'Laughlin, Margaret —26
Olsen, Merlin —100, 107
Ousterhout —22, 23

P

Parr, Bill —40
Patterson, Charles —88
Patton, James —35, 51
Perilman, Abe —xiii, xv, 6, 64, 65, 67, 68, 69, 86, 87, 91, 93, 96, 98
Perry, Alan —vii
Perry, Cindy —vii
Perry, Dan —vii, xi, xvi, 6, 138, 139, 140, 141
Perry, Irene —viii, 140
Peterson, Bob —84
Pettes, Charles — xii, 75, 79, 113
Phelps, Ruth —25
Pilot, James 'Preacher' —113, 125, 128
Pratt, Lemuel —38, 39, 40, 41
Presley, Early —84
Priestley, Orville — 6, 63
Pruitt, Berley —65
Pusateri, John —79

Q

Quesenberry, Fred —27
Quesenberry, Joe —23, 24, 25, 27, 28

R

Ralston, John —109
Rea (Miss) —25
Read, Don —131
Ream, Marlen —79
Reese, Ernie —110
Rentfrow, Doyle —25, 27, 28

INDEX

R (continued)
Rentfrow, Era —23, 24, 25, 26, 121
Rentfrow, Dette (Bendette) —13, 24, 25, 26
Richardson, Derrick —128
Rierson, Don — xii, 114
Rockne, Knute —22
Robbins —22, 25
Roberts, Don —79
Rodich, Jerry —116, 140
Rodriguez, Manny —128
Rogers, Charlie —vii, viii. xv, 1, 139, 141
Rogers, Taveon —128
Rooney, Mickey—40
Roosevelt, Franklin D. —33, 63
Roosevelt, Teddy —121
Rosewall, Ken —87
Rudzik, Dick—75, 79, 139
Russell, Clarence W. —13, 18, 27
Rust, Rob '84
Rutherford, Mike — xii

S
Saban, Nick —10, 128
Samuel, Tony —125, 126, 127
Savage, Antony —13, 15
Savage, Arthur J. 'Dutch' —13
Sears, Art —55
Sepkowitz, Allan — xii, 70, 75, 79, 92, 113, 130, 139, 142
Shamburg, John — xii, 79, 83, 85, 113, 143
Skinner, Harry —40, 72
Simpson, O.J. —61
Sims, E.A. — xii, 64, 73, 75, 81, 82, 83, 88, 90, 91, 100, 102, 105, 108, 110, 113, 114, 130, 143
Sinnock, W.P. —13
Skipworth, Roy —xiv
Smith, Reese —57, 84
Smolanovich, Pete — xii, 87, 88, 97, 113, 130, 139
Snow, O.C. —11, 12
Snyder, Bill —135
Spanogle, Mark —39, 40

Squires, —15
Stagg, Amos Alonzo —10
Stephens, Harold —102
Steward, Alice —26
Stewart, Jimmy —40
Strickland, Floyd — xii, 70, 76, 89, 90, 99, 113
Strong, Vida —26
Sutherland, William —10, 13, 14, 17

T
Tackett, Jim —51
Taft, William —14
Teaff, Grant —91
Teresa, Mother —121
Terrell, Roy —129
Thayer, Frank —viii, 1, 139, 141
Thaxton, Robert —28
Tingley, Clyde —36, 41, 43
Thompson, Charles —79
Thompson, Dave — xii, 79, 102, 110, 113, 130, 139, 143
Thorpe, Jim —85
Tombaugh, Clyde —6
Tubb, Gary —79

V
Veazey, Doug — xii, 70, 75, 79, 86, 113, 143
Vickers —22
Villalobos, Alejandro —84
Villanueva, Danny —74, 75, 79
Villanueva, Jim —75, 139

W
Waldner, Mike —viii, 1, 139, 140, 141
Waldner, Nancy —140
Walker, Dwayne —36, 125, 126
Wallace, Bill — xii, 68, 75, 79, 90, 100, 113, 130, 139
Wallace, Jewell —68
Warmath, Murray —118
Wayne, Clayborn (Clayborne) —40, 41
Webb, Jimmy —93

INDEX

Weeks, Bill —84, 89, 116
West, Mae —111
White, Charles —61
White, Howard —83, 03
Whitlock, Chuck —92, 103
Williams, Chris —128
Williams, Dan —36
Williams, Joe —79
Wilson, Woodrow —27, 121
Winslow, Bob —60, 61
Witt, J.W. — xii, 70, 71, 73, 75, 79, 83, 85, 100, 113, 115, 116, 130, 139, 143
Wood, Jim —117, 125, 126
Wood, Wayne —79
Womack, Randy —67
Woodson, Dawn —118, 138
Woodson, Muriel —118
Woodson, Warren — xi, xiv, xvi, 1, 21, 23, 33, 34, 35, 36, 48, 55, 56, 57, 58, 59, 60, 61, 62, 63, 64, 65, 66, 67, 68, 69, 70, 72, 73, 76, 77, 79, 81, 82, 83, 84, 86, 90, 91, 93, 95, 97, 98, 99, 102, 104, 107, 109, 113, 114, 115, 116, 117, 118, 121, 122, 125, 126, 127, 128, 129, 130, 131, 132, 133, 137, 138, 139, 140
Worrick, Jim — xii, 65, 70, 113, 114, 129, 139, 143

Y

Yannessa, Don — xii, 70, 76, 79, 83, 87, 91, 100, 113, 129, 139, 143
Yelvington, Browning — xii, 67, 76, 79, 129, 139
Young, Ray —96
Yurcic, Joe —39, 41, 42

Z

Zechman, Fred —125, 126
Zivkovich, Lou — xii, 71, 73, 75, 78, 81, 91, 96, 97, 102, 111, 113, 114, 129, 143
Zuger, Joe —98